...the guest is not
to scratch
himself in
company, not to
blow in his soup,
not to return
the meat to the
dish after
smelling it. He
must not pocket
the fruit at
dessert, and he
must not
put a second
morsel into
his mouth before
the first
has been
swallowed.

—*The Customs of Mankind*, ©1924

This book is dedicated to Nunzio James Cimino.

First Edition
16 15 14 13 12 5 4 3 2 1

Published by
Gibbs Smith
P.O. Box 667
Layton, Utah 84041
1.800.835.4993 orders
www.gibbs-smith.com

Designed by Drew Furlong
Printed and bound in Hong Kong

Gibbs Smith books are printed on either recycled, 100% post-consumer waste, FSC-certified papers or on paper produced from sustainable PEFC-certified forest/controlled wood source. Learn more at www.pefc.org.

Library of Congress Cataloging-in-Publication Data

Cook, Cristina Ceccatelli.
Cristina's of Sun Valley con gusto! / Cristina Ceccatelli Cook ; photography by Kirsten Shultz. — First edition.
pages cm
Includes index.
ISBN 978-1-4236-3189-7
1. Cooking, Italian. 2. Cristina's Restaurant. I. Title.
TX723.C6345 2013
641.5945—dc23
2012024550

con gusto!

cristina's

of sun valley

Cristina Ceccatelli Cook

photography by Kirsten Shultz

GIBBS SMITH

TO ENRICH AND INSPIRE HUMANKIND

contents

acknowledgments

Special thanks to my loyal and fascinating customers, who continue to expand our horizons and make Cristina's such a lively place;

To our local farmers and ranchers, who bring us the freshest organic products despite the challenges of Rocky Mountain weather;

To the professional "magicians" whose frequent repairs keep this old Ketchum house from falling apart;

To Patrick Jam, Michael White, Raylene Ward, and their kitchen team for their inspired cooking;

To Diane Hull and her bakers Lila, Guadalupe, and Lyndi, who create our beautiful breads, pastries, and desserts;

To front staff manager Magaly Estrada and her team of Juan, Paul, Rian, Mihai, Niki, Brennan, Sam, and Cameron, who roam the front of the restaurant and tell our customers, "Anything is possible here";

To Cecelia Muñoz, our unflappable office manager, without whom there would be total chaos;

To my son, Christopher, who says, "As your attorney, Mom, I suggest you try to exercise your right to remain silent";

To my editor, Karen Oswalt, for listening to my ramblings, organizing my thoughts, and traveling with me on this adventure.

CRISTINA'S
RESTAURANT
BAKERY
TAKE AWAY
CATERING
520 SECOND STREET EAST • 726 4499

foreword

Cristina reminds me of all the great chefs I have known. Everything that distinguishes them, she embodies. Her gifts, like theirs, are far greater than just cooking. First and foremost, she has passion for what she does and the great taste to match the passion. She has dedicated a lifetime to learning about traditions, ingredients, and techniques. Coupled with that is how intuitive she is. She just knows. Because she makes it all look so effortless, it is easy to overlook her professionalism.

All of my adult life I have lived in Las Vegas, a place where imagination and exaggeration run wild. The resorts are expansive. The scale and size of the rooms are large, the production shows are lavish, extensive shopping can be found on every corner, and world-class events occur on a regular basis. When restaurants became part of the entertainment scene across the globe, wonderful restaurants were added to the menu of choices available in Las Vegas. Only such a unique place—which has forever been dedicated to satisfying "appetites"—could have assembled the finest collection of chefs in the world.

In the last 20 years, I have been privileged to work with many of Las Vegas's marvelous chefs and to have been fed by the rest. I am grateful to all of them for making my palate more sophisticated and my dining more pleasurable than even I imagined!

For all of us who cherish Sun Valley and its wholesome mountain lifestyle, we are blessed not to have to compromise when it comes to food. We have the glorious talents of Cristina and her marvelous restaurant. Not only is she a true treasure, she has been my private Idaho jewel. Knowing that I can have her in my own kitchen is a luxury that fulfills my own fantasies! Whether she is preparing hors d'oeuvres for a cocktail party, an intimate dinner for my dearest friends, or the most sentimental family holiday meal, I am completely confident that all will be flawless—and delicious!

—Elaine Wynn
Director, Wynn Resorts

CRISTINA'S RESTAURANT

ciao amore

When people ask me how Cristina's of Sun Valley came to be, I think of my mother at the door of our old farmhouse, saying, *"Ciao amore."* She said that to me twice a year for 20 years as I left to go back to America. Her words expressed all the truths, the aspirations, and the apprehensions that a mother and daughter share. I was traveling to a land unknown to her. She hoped to see me again but was not sure she would.

Ciao amore (literally, "hello, love; good-bye, love") is a phrase that defies translation. Depending upon how you say it—your inflection, your body language, and to whom you say it—it can mean many things. In my mother's case, it meant she gave me permission to go off far away.

I turned 60 this year, and looking back I realize that my life has been like a collage—a piece here, a piece there. Many times I have found myself asking, Did I really do that? I have always operated on the power of gut feelings. When you know something to be right. I have heard the whispers telling me to conform, to fit in. But I have never been able to subscribe to the conventional way of doing things. Instead, I have lived, as we say, *con gusto*—taking risks, exploring, doing things I could hardly imagine. That is the answer as to how this restaurant came about!

I like to think of my restaurant not as a business but as a cozy place—intimate, busy, loud at times, like the traditional *trattorie* I grew up with. Filled with customers whose eccentricity is surpassed only by their laughter. The tables may be plain and worn by 20 years of use, they may be covered with white linens at times, but they are always warm and inviting. The house wine is always good and the food has a timeless and comforting quality of a meal you might prepare in your own home. It is a place where you can feel comfortable dipping crusts of bread into pools of delicious sauce.

We Florentines don't worry too much about calories. We are real *golosi*—passionate about our food, *particolari* about gelato. We like *fatto a mano* (made by hand), these days in a new way, with curiosity and creativity. We weave the old into the new. We dream about *soffritto* (sautéed things) and we smash pitted olives, we spice them up with peperoncino, and guess what we call them? *Le olive dell'amore!*

Our customers come and go. We welcome them to our table and we say good-bye when they leave. The restaurant is more than the food, more than the wine and the tables; it is who we are.

I think of my mother and *ciao amore.*

—Cristina

antipasti

marinated artichoke hearts

6 to 7 pieces

- 1 can (14 ounces) whole artichoke hearts in water, drained
- pinch of freshly cracked black pepper
- 2 bay leaves
- zest and juice of ¼ lemon
- 1 tablespoon white wine vinegar
- 2½ tablespoons extra virgin olive oil

In a bowl, toss all ingredients together.

Antipasti *are one of Italy's most gracious cultural traditions. From the Latin* ante *(before) and* pastum *(food), their purpose is to entice the appetite before the main meal. They originated during the Renaissance, when lavish banquets both began and ended with delicate cold dishes of sweet and savory flavors. From* affetati misti *(assorted cured meats) to anchovies, olives to marinated artichokes, fresh and dried fruits to delicious bites of seafood . . .* bruschette, crostini, pizzette *. . . little has changed.* Prosciutto *is thinly sliced by hand and served with melon or figs;* bresaola *is served with a drizzle of extra virgin olive oil, a squeeze of lemon juice, and freshly cracked black pepper. And let us not forget the endless varieties of* salami *from Tuscany and Umbria. Cheese was typically served by the Etruscans, who introduced* fior di latte, pecorino *with fava beans and salt, and assorted other cheeses, including creamy, aged, blue. But then, of course, the question arises, How much cheese can a person eat?*

prosciutto cones

serves 6

6 slices prosciutto

4 ounces young watercress

4 ounces pecorino toscano, cut in matchsticks

freshly cracked black pepper

Place prosciutto slices on a cutting board. Arrange watercress and cheese matchsticks on top, and roll prosciutto into the shape of a cone so the watercress and cheese stick out the top.

Lightly coat a serving plate with mustard-chive vinaigrette. Arrange prosciutto cones seam side down on top. Drizzle with a little more vinaigrette, add freshly cracked pepper and serve.

mustard-chive vinaigrette

makes about 1/2 cup

6 chives, minced

1 teaspoon crushed mustard seeds

juice of 1/2 lemon

1/4 cup extra virgin olive oil

pinch of salt

Whisk together chives, mustard seeds, and lemon juice in a small mixing bowl. Slowly add olive oil and whisk until mixture reaches a creamy consistency. Whisk in salt and adjust to taste.

poached pears

makes 6

3 cups orange juice

3 cups white wine

1 cinnamon stick, 2 whole cloves, 2 star anise (optional)

6 very firm bartlett pears

2 tablespoons honey

In a saucepan, combine the orange juice and white wine. If you like, add spices.

Peel the pears and place in the saucepan. Add a little water to cover the pears if the wine and juice do not. Cut a piece of parchment paper to fit the top of the pan and gently press just to the top of the liquid.

On low heat, bring the pears to a simmer. Check after 25 minutes. When you can easily pierce the pears with a toothpick, they are done. Remove pears from the poaching liquid and set aside to cool. Reduce poaching liquid to 1 cup. Add 2 tablespoons of honey for sweetness and shine.

Serve the pears drizzled with the honey glaze and accompanied by your favorite cheese. Or dip the pears in ganache (p. 171) and toasted almonds for dessert. They are also good sliced in salads.

There is a Tuscan saying, "Never let the peasants know how good cheese is with pears!" We all know that the sweetness of the pears combined with the milky taste of the cheese is the best. We like it for antipasto, we like it for lunch, we like it for an afternoon snack—and we also like it for dessert.

tuscan liver crostini

makes 12 to 14

4 tablespoons extra virgin olive oil

1/2 cup diced yellow onion

8 ounces chicken livers, membranes removed

2 bay leaves

3 juniper berries

1 tablespoon capers, plus extra for garnish

2 anchovy fillets (optional)

1/3 cup madeira

1/3 cup white wine

1/4 cup chicken broth

freshly cracked black pepper

1 baguette, sliced and lightly toasted

1 egg white, cooked and chopped, for garnish

pinch of finely chopped italian parsley, for garnish

extra virgin olive oil

In a sauté pan, heat olive oil over medium-low heat and sauté onions until soft and golden. Add chicken livers, bay leaves, juniper berries, 1 tablespoon capers, and anchovies, and cook over high heat for a few minutes, stirring occasionally. Add the madeira and white wine to deglaze. Add broth and freshly cracked black pepper, reduce heat, and cook a few more minutes. Keep the mixture very moist, and do not reduce all the liquid. Remove from pan to a cutting board and finely chop.

Preheat oven to broil.

Top baguette slices with a dollop of the chicken liver mixture. Place on a baking sheet and broil a few minutes, until edges of the bread are crispy. Serve garnished with chopped egg white, a caper or two, a pinch of parsley, and a drizzle of olive oil and broth if needed.

If you do not use the liver mixture immediately, you can store it up to 3 days. Just add more chicken broth to moisten.

goat cheese with cassis onions

makes about 1 cup

- 1 large red onion, diced (about 2½ cups)
- 1 tablespoon extra virgin olive oil
- salt and pepper
- ¾ cup crème de cassis
- ¼ cup red wine vinegar
- 1 tablespoon sugar
- 1 (8-ounce) fresh goat cheese log
- pinch of fresh thyme
- flatbreads, ciabatta, or focaccia

In a large sauté pan over medium heat, sauté onions in olive oil with salt and pepper to taste until golden and translucent, about 8 minutes. Add crème de cassis and red wine vinegar, and cook until alcohol evaporates and onions are shiny, about 4 minutes. Stir in sugar and cook 1 minute. Remove from heat and set aside.

Slice goat cheese into ½-inch rounds.* Broil for 30 seconds on an ungreased baking sheet.

Place cheese rounds on a serving plate and loosely arrange onions on top. Sprinkle with thyme and serve with flatbreads, ciabatta, or focaccia.

*Goat cheese logs are easy to cut with a fishing line or a cheese cutter.

crackerbread

makes 6 or 7

- ½ teaspoon active dry yeast
- 1 ½ cups warm water
- 1 tablespoon honey
- 2 teaspoons apple cider vinegar
- ½ teaspoon salt
- 2 cups whole wheat flour
- ½ cup unbleached all-purpose flour
- ½ cup rye flour
- 1 tablespoon extra virgin olive oil
- grated parmigiano, sesame seeds, or herbs (optional)
- salt and pepper

Preheat oven to 350° F.

In the bowl of a stand mixer with a dough hook, dissolve yeast in warm water. Add honey, vinegar, salt, flours, and olive oil and mix on low speed about 3 minutes, then on medium speed for 5 minutes.

On a lightly floured surface, divide dough into 6 or 7 balls. Roll dough into thin ovals 12 to 13 inches in diameter. If you like, sprinkle with parmigiano or sesame seeds and salt and pepper. Bake on a cookie sheet lined with parchment paper on the lower rack for 15 to 20 minutes, rotating the pan a few times while baking, until crackerbread is golden brown. Repeat until all dough is used. Remove and let cool on a rack. Crackerbread should be crunchy.

salmon cakes

makes 36

- 2 pounds fresh wild salmon
- 1/2 teaspoon salt
- 1/4 teaspoon pepper
- extra virgin olive oil
- zest of 2 lemons, juice reserved
- 4 green onions, finely chopped (about 1 cup)
- 3 stalks tender celery hearts with leaves, finely chopped (about 1 cup)
- 1 fresh red cayenne pepper, minced, or 1/2 teaspoon dried cayenne
- 1 teaspoon old bay seasoning
- 2 cups finely ground breadcrumbs, divided in half
- 2 eggs
- 3 tablespoons clarified butter* or vegetable oil for frying

Preheat oven to 475° F.

Place salmon skin side down on a baking sheet lined with aluminum foil and sprinkle with salt and pepper. Rub with a little olive oil. Bake on lower rack until salmon is partially cooked, about 8 minutes. Using a spatula, remove from baking sheet, discarding skin, and set aside to cool.

In a mixing bowl, combine the lemon zest, green onion, celery, cayenne, old bay, 1 cup breadcrumbs, and eggs and stir with a fork. Flake the cooked salmon and add to the mixture.

Shape the salmon mixture into 36 cakes, about 1 ounce each. Place the remaining breadcrumbs on a plate or waxed paper and dip both sides in the crumbs. Refrigerate 10 minutes.

In a wide-bottomed sauté pan over medium heat, add the clarified butter or vegetable oil. Working quickly, brown the cakes on both sides. Repeat until all cakes are browned. This can be done up to one day ahead.

When ready to serve, place the salmon cakes on a baking sheet lined with parchment paper and bake at 500° F. for 1 to 2 minutes to crisp. Serve with a squeeze of fresh lemon juice and green goddess dressing (p. 29).

*To make clarified butter, melt 2 sticks of unsalted butter on low heat. As the butter simmers gently, skim the foam off the surface until the butter is clear. Pour into a glass container, leaving the solids on the bottom of the pan. Store in the refrigerator for up to 3 months.

green goddess dressing

makes 2½ cups

2 cloves garlic
1 cup coarsely chopped green onion
1 cup chopped italian parsley
1 cup mayonnaise
1 cup sour cream
1 tablespoon red wine vinegar
pinch of salt and pepper

In a food processor, pulse garlic, green onions, and parsley 10 to 15 times. Do not purée. Add the mayonnaise, sour cream, and vinegar and pulse again until ingredients are semi-smooth. Season with salt and pepper.

Green goddess is great as a dip, as a dressing for salads, or as a sandwich spread. It will last 7 to 10 days in the refrigerator.

grilled pizza with pears, pecorino and walnuts

makes three 12-inch pizzas

8 ounces toscano fresco

1½ ripe pears, thinly sliced

½ cup walnut pieces, coarsely chopped

extra virgin olive oil

freshly cracked black pepper

Thinly slice toscano fresco and arrange atop prepared skins (p. 33). Cover with a single layer of pear slices, then scatter walnuts over top.

Heat grill to medium. Transfer pizzas to grill or a pizza stone in a 400° F. oven, and cook until cheese is soft and crust is lightly browned on the bottom.

Transfer pizzas to a wooden board. Sprinkle with pepper and drizzle with oil. Cut into wedges and serve.

pizza skins

makes ten 12-inch skins

1/2 tablespoon active dry yeast

2 1/4 cups warm water

5 cups italian flour (or substitute unbleached all-purpose flour)

1 tablespoon salt

1/2 cup flour, for dusting and rolling skins

In the bowl of a stand mixer with a paddle attachment, dissolve yeast in the warm water. Add flour and salt. Mix until dough clumps together, about 3 minutes. Transfer to a lightly floured surface and knead for about 5 minutes, or until dough is soft and elastic. Place in a bowl, dust with flour, cover with a kitchen towel, and let rest in a warm place for at least 1 hour, or until doubled in volume.

Punch down the dough to its original size, then transfer to a lightly floured surface. Divide the dough into 10 balls, dust with flour, cover with a towel, and let rest for about 30 minutes. Working with one ball at a time, flatten the dough to form a circle. Using the heel of your hand and working from the center of the ball outwards, or using a rolling pin, stretch it as much as you can, dusting with flour as you go to form a 12-inch skin.

Partially cook the skins for about 1 minute either on the grill or in a 550° F. oven.

Extras can be wrapped in plastic and frozen for later use.

We Italians say that pizza satisfies both dignity and hunger, because whether you are rich or poor, you can have a great meal. As for me, I am in love—in love with pizza! Thin, crunchy, and with a very small amount of fresh toppings.

wheat gluten-free pizza skins

makes six 11-inch skins

- 1½ cups warm water
- 1 tablespoon active dry yeast
- 4 teaspoons sugar
- 2 cups bob's red mill wheat gluten-free all-purpose flour
- 1 cup cornstarch
- ¼ cup potato starch
- 4 teaspoons xanthan gum
- 1 teaspoon salt
- 2 tablespoons extra virgin olive oil
- ½ cup rice flour, for rolling

Preheat oven with pizza stone to 500° F.

In a bowl, combine water, yeast, and sugar until dissolved and bubbling. Set aside.

In the bowl of a stand mixer with a paddle attachment, mix flour, cornstarch, potato starch, xanthan gum, and salt. Add the yeast mixture and olive oil and mix on medium speed for about 8 minutes.

Transfer dough to a generously floured surface and shape into six 4½-ounce balls. Roll into 11-inch circles. Dough will be very soft and sticky, so use plenty of rice flour while handling and shaping. If dough tears, patch and press together and don't worry about it!

Bake on a hot pizza stone for 1 minute, until skin bubbles.

Remove skins with a spatula and top with your favorite topping. Return to oven until crisp, about 2 minutes.

Michel is a French restaurateur in Ketchum. As everyone knows, the French and the Italians argue about everything—from soccer to wine to women and men. Somehow, Michel and I have been able to manage our differences and to laugh over pommes frites!

bruschetta of strawberries & tomatoes

makes 3 1/2 cups

2 cups strawberries, quartered
1 1/2 cups sweet cherry tomatoes, quartered
1/2 cup fresh basil chiffonade
1 tablespoon extra virgin olive oil
3 tablespoons agreste*
salt and freshly cracked black pepper
grilled ciabatta slices

Gently toss ingredients together. Serve on slices of grilled ciabatta.

**Agreste* is a tart, green grape juice made by pressing the grapes before they ripen. It can be found in specialty stores.

salads

spinach, artichoke & roasted beet salad

serves 6 to 8

1 1/2 pounds gold beets

2 (14-ounce) cans artichoke hearts, drained

1 tablespoon extra virgin olive oil

1/2 pound baby spinach, long stems removed

1 1/2 cups cristina's spicy nuts

1/4 pound shaved montasio cheese

salt and pepper

Cook beets in cold salted water until tender. Drain and let cool before removing skins.

Preheat oven to 500° F.

Cut beets in wedges and place on a baking sheet. Cut artichokes in half and add to baking sheet. Drizzle with olive oil and roast about 20 minutes. Remove from oven and set aside.

In a large bowl, toss baby spinach with beets, artichokes, and a splash of lemon vinaigrette. Plate and sprinkle with spicy nuts. Top with shaved cheese and salt and pepper to taste.

I believe in lunch. Not a quick bite at the mall, but Lunch. We can't all become psychiatrists to discover our inner selves, but we know one thing for sure: we all need company and we all need to express our feelings. Over lunch we share not just wine and bread but also our joys, our worries, our secrets. A good lunch should provide great food as well as a spirit of conviviality, enjoyment, and gusto!

lemon vinaigrette

makes 1 cup

1/2 cup extra virgin olive oil

1/2 cup freshly squeezed lemon juice

1/2 cup finely chopped italian parsley

1 tablespoon brown sugar

salt and pepper

Whisk together all ingredients.

Lemon vinaigrette is good warm or cold, on fish, salads, chicken, or fruit.

cristina's spicy nuts

makes 2 cups

1/2 cup sugar

2 tablespoons vegetable oil

2 cups unsalted mixed nuts—pecans, hazelnuts, almonds, cashews, walnuts, brazil nuts

1 1/2 teaspoons cumin

1/2 teaspoon red pepper flakes

In a sauté pan over low heat, stir sugar and oil with a wooden spoon until sugar is completely dissolved. Add nuts, cumin, and red pepper flakes. Toss with the sugar syrup until mixture is golden brown, making sure nuts are completely coated.

Transfer the hot mixture onto a lightly greased cookie sheet, spread, and let cool. When nuts have cooled, break apart with a wooden spoon.

ketchy salad

serves 6

12 quail eggs

1 tablespoon salt

2 heads romaine hearts, separated and left whole

4 cups baby spinach

3 cups mâche

1/2 pound gruyère, thinly sliced and cut in strips

1/2 pound parma cotto ham, thinly sliced and cut in strips

1/2 sweet onion, thinly sliced

Place uncooked quail eggs in enough cold salted water to cover. Bring to a boil. Remove from heat, cover, and let stand for 4 minutes. Rinse in cold water and peel.

Plate the romaine hearts, then add the spinach and mâche. Arrange the gruyère, ham, onion, and halved quail eggs in individual clusters around the greens. Just before serving, dress with french dressing.

french dressing

makes 2 1/2 cups

1 tablespoon extra virgin olive oil

1 tablespoon finely diced shallot

1 tablespoon honey

1/2 teaspoon paprika

1 cup white wine vinegar

1/4 cup chopped yellow onion

1 teaspoon dijon mustard

1 cup vegetable oil

1/4 cup extra virgin olive oil

1/4 teaspoon salt

1 tablespoon chopped chives

In a small saucepan over medium heat, bring first 4 ingredients to simmer. Stir in white wine vinegar and set aside.

In a food processor with a blade attachment, blend onion, mustard, vegetable oil, olive oil, and salt until smooth. Whisk in vinegar mixture and chives.

When I am in Italy, I always have lunch with my friend Rita at the Caffè Michelangelo in Piazza Ferrucci Oltrarno—literally, over the Arno—in a part of Florence that is home to artists, artisans, and everyday working people. Walking into the caffè, I can't resist looking at the display cases bursting with pasticcini, focaccie, tramezzini, dolcezze *. . . and the well-dressed businessmen at lunch with their* aperitivi *or* cappuccini, *checking out the women. I miss it. We sit outside surrounded by the bustle of the cars, buses, and vespas. The river is right there. I am home. The white-shirted* barrista *knows I am not a regular and offers me wine and a menu. Rita is old news. We order, and as the words and laughter flow, we eat a salad like this. It is a good lunch. Before leaving we share two more things: the last book we read and the last man we wanted to kiss. We still love life, and Florence brings it out.* "Ciao, bella! A presto!"

pears & grapes with sottocenere al tartufo

serves 6

juice of 1 lemon

2 cups cold water

3 ripe bartlett pears

2 cups white seedless grapes, sliced in 1/8-inch rounds

1 cup whole parsley leaves

1/2 cup walnut pieces

3 tablespoons white balsamic vinegar

2 tablespoons extra virgin olive oil

1/3 pound sottocenere al tartufo,* shaved

In a bowl, put lemon juice and cold water. Peel the pears and cut in 1/2-inch cubes. Place the pears in the lemon water for 5 minutes to keep them from turning color. Drain.

In a separate bowl, combine grapes, parsley, walnuts, and pears. Toss with vinegar and olive oil. Serve with the shaved cheese.

*Sottocenere al tartufo *is a pale, mild cheese mixed with truffles and aged in ashes to preserve it and infuse it with flavor.*

We call truffles the diamonds of the forest. In Umbria and Piemonte, fall is truffle season. People taste, gossip, and boast about their dogs, who can sniff out truffles from a distance.

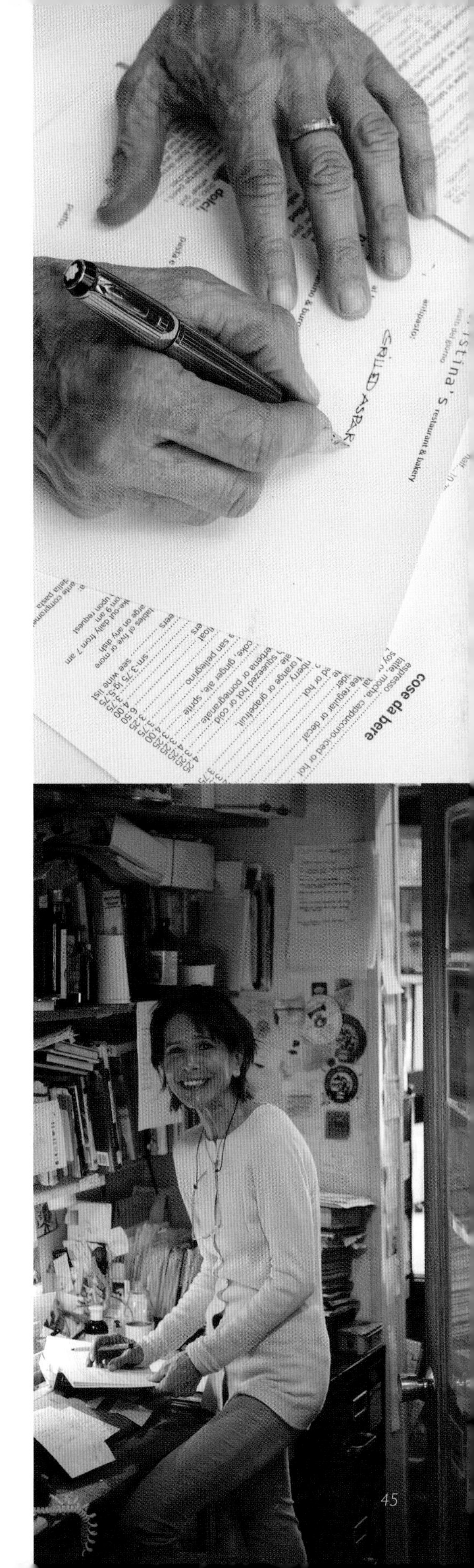

classic macaroni salad

serves 8

1/2 pound macaroni, cooked al dente

1 cup spanish green olives, sliced in rounds

1/2 cup white cheddar cheese, cut in small cubes

1 1/2 cups prosciutto cotto (1/2 pound), cut in small cubes

1 1/2 cups finely chopped celery hearts and leaves

1/2 cup cornichons, sliced in rounds

1/4 cup chopped italian parsley

2 teaspoons red wine vinegar

salt and pepper

In a large mixing bowl, combine all ingredients and set aside while you prepare the lemon alioli.

Add half the lemon alioli to the macaroni salad and taste. Add more alioli if desired, or save the rest for later.

lemon alioli

makes 1 cup

1 egg yolk

1 whole egg

1 clove garlic

juice of 1 lemon

2/3 cup extra virgin olive oil

In a food processor with a blade attachment, blend egg, garlic, and lemon juice. On low speed, add the olive oil in a slow stream. When oil has been added, blend mixture on high for a few seconds, until alioli is thick and creamy.

insalatina tiepida

serves 6

13 ounces apple smoked bacon, chopped

1 pound mixed greens

6 radishes, thinly sliced

1 cup croutons

1 pound asparagus, trimmed, blanched, and julienned

1/2 pound grape tomatoes, cubed

6 eggs

extra virgin olive oil

salt and freshly cracked black pepper

6 pieces toasted country bread

In a skillet, sauté the bacon on medium-low heat until crispy. Drain, reserving bacon drippings. Set aside and keep warm.

Divide greens into 6 bowls. Arrange radishes, croutons, asparagus, tomatoes, and bacon on each salad.

Poach the eggs.

Top each salad with a poached egg. Drizzle with warm bacon drippings and olive oil. Season with salt and freshly cracked black pepper. Serve with toasted bread.

poached eggs

Fill a large, wide pan almost to the rim with water, add a drop of white vinegar, and bring to a low boil. Drop 2 to 4 eggs at a time into the boiling water and cook 2 1/2 minutes for soft, or to your taste.

Eggs are an inexhaustible source of light, nutritious dishes. In Florence, we like to eat them for antipasto, lunch, or dinner. If the eggs come from your own chickens—so much the better!

three-color salad

serves 6

1 red endive, thinly sliced lengthwise with core intact

4 cups arugula

2 heads butterleaf, white hearts only

2 large navel oranges, cut in segments

2 ripe avocados

salt and pepper

In a large bowl, toss the endive, arugula, butterleaf, and orange segments with a pinch of salt. Slice the avocados in half and remove the pits. Cut the avocados in 1/4-inch slices. Arrange the greens and oranges on 6 plates. Place 4 or 5 slices of avocado on each salad and drizzle with orange-balsamic vinegar. Add salt and pepper to taste. If you cannot find this vinegar in the gourmet section of your grocery, you can use the recipe below.

orange-balsamic vinegar

makes 1/2 cup

1/2 cup white balsamic vinegar

1/2 cup orange juice

1/4 cup sugar

In a small saucepan on simmer, reduce ingredients for 8 to 10 minutes. Chill before using.

wilted escarole, chicken & charred tomato salad

serves 6

- 3 tablespoons extra virgin olive oil, plus extra for cooking
- 1 tablespoon fresh oregano leaves
- 1 tablespoon fresh thyme leaves
- 4 cloves garlic, minced
- 1 teaspoon salt
- 1/2 teaspoon coarsely ground black pepper
- 6 roma tomatoes, halved
- 6 boneless, skinless chicken breasts (about 2 pounds), pounded 1/2 inch thick
- 1 large red onion, cut in 1/4-inch rounds
- 3 heads escarole, split in half with core intact
- 1/4 pound istara cheese, shaved

In a large mixing bowl, combine 3 tablespoons olive oil, oregano, thyme, garlic, salt, and pepper. Add the tomato halves and stir to coat, then remove and set aside. Marinate chicken in remaining herb/oil mixture.

In a large cast-iron skillet coated with olive oil over medium-high heat, cook the sliced onion 8 minutes on each side, keeping it in rounds. Onions should be soft and slightly charred. Remove onions and set aside.

Turn the same skillet to high heat. Cook the tomatoes cut side down for 3 minutes, then turn and cook for 2 minutes on the skin side. Remove tomatoes and set aside. Add a little olive oil and reduce heat to medium. Add the chicken breasts and cook for 3 minutes on each side. Remove chicken to a cutting board.

Preheat oven to high broil. Place the escarole on a baking sheet and drizzle with a little olive oil and a pinch of salt and pepper. Broil until wilted.

To serve, layer escarole, tomatoes, onions, chicken, and cheese. Drizzle with cobb vinaigrette.

cobb vinaigrette

makes 2 cups

- 1/2 cup water
- 1/2 cup red wine vinegar
- 1/2 teaspoon sugar
- juice of 1/2 lemon
- 1 teaspoon salt
- 1/2 teaspoon freshly cracked black pepper
- 1 1/2 teaspoons worcestershire sauce
- 1/2 teaspoon dijon mustard
- 1 clove garlic, minced
- 3/4 cup extra virgin olive oil

Whisk ingredients together until blended.

quinoa salad

serves 8

2 cups quinoa

4½ cups water

pinch of salt

1½ cups sugar peas, blanched for 1 minute and julienned

2 or 3 radishes, sliced paper-thin

½ red bell pepper, julienned (about 1 cup)

1 small carrot, julienned (about 1 cup)

½ cup red onion, sliced in paper-thin crescents and sprinkled with 1 tablespoon sugar

2 cups fresh watercress, larger stems removed

½ cup ricotta salata, crumbled

In a strainer, rinse quinoa in cold water.

In a saucepan, place quinoa in 4½ cups cold water with a pinch of salt. Bring to a boil, then reduce heat, cover, and simmer 20 minutes. The grain will look soft and translucent and will display a little tail. Drain but do not rinse. Cool on a baking sheet.

In a large mixing bowl, combine quinoa, sugar peas, radishes, bell pepper, carrot, and red onion. Refrigerate.

To serve, toss salad in lemon-mint dressing, and serve on a bed of watercress. Top with ricotta salata.

lemon-mint dressing

makes ½ cup

3 tablespoons lemon juice

½ cup chopped mint

1 clove garlic, minced

2 tablespoons extra virgin olive oil

1 teaspoon kosher salt

½ teaspoon freshly ground black pepper

In a small mixing bowl, whisk ingredients together. Refrigerate separately from the quinoa until ready to serve.

Quinoa has a mild, nutty flavor and is often used as a grain, although it is actually a member of the spinach family. It is easy to cook, but don't forget to rinse the seeds well to remove the bitter coating that protects them from birds.

soups & stews

chicken with kale & chickpeas

serves 8 to 10

chicken stock

1 whole chicken, about 4 pounds

1 yellow onion, coarsely chopped

2 carrots, peeled and coarsely chopped

2 stalks celery, coarsely chopped

3 bay leaves

3 whole cloves garlic

1/2 teaspoon peppercorns

1/2 teaspoon fennel seeds

6 juniper berries

1 1/2 tablespoons salt

6 quarts cold water

In a soup pot, place chicken and all ingredients. Bring to a boil, then reduce heat and simmer partially covered for 35 minutes, or until chicken is just cooked.

Remove chicken from broth and transfer to a bowl to cool. When the chicken is cool enough to handle, remove the meat from the bones and shred. Return bones and skin to the pot. Continue to simmer the broth and vegetables uncovered for 20 to 30 minutes while you prepare the other vegetables for the soup.

vegetables

1 large yellow onion, cut in thin crescents

2 large carrots, peeled and diced

2 stalks celery, diced

1 tablespoon minced garlic

1 zucchini, cut in 1/2 rounds

1 yellow squash, cut in 1/2 rounds

1 (14-ounce) can chickpeas, drained and rinsed

5 roma tomatoes, chopped

3/4 teaspoon each tarragon, basil, and oregano

1 tablespoon soy sauce

3 cups coarsely chopped italian black kale

salt and pepper

grated parmigiano

Strain the chicken broth into a soup pot, then add the onion, carrot, and celery, and simmer for about 15 minutes. Add the remaining ingredients except for the chicken, kale, and parmigiano, and simmer for 35 minutes. Add the chicken and kale, and simmer 10 more minutes. Season to taste with salt and pepper. Serve with grated parmigiano.

lobster bisque

serves 8 to 10

- 8 cups lobster broth (or lobster concentrate)
- 1 quart heavy whipping cream
- 1 cup minced celery
- 1 cup minced red onion
- 1 1/2 cups thinly sliced leeks, white part only, cut in half rounds
- 1/4 pound unsalted butter
- 1 cup dry sherry
- 3/4 cup unbleached all-purpose flour
- 3 bay leaves
- 1/2 tablespoon tarragon
- 1 teaspoon celery seed
- 2 tablespoons chopped italian parsley
- 2 tablespoons chopped fresh dill
- 1/2 fresh vanilla bean, split
- 2 pounds lobster claw and knuckle meat, cooked
- oyster crackers and fresh chives, for garnish

In a saucepan, bring lobster broth and cream to a slow simmer.

In a large pot over medium heat, cook celery, onion, leeks, and butter for about 15 minutes. Add the sherry and cook until evaporated. Add the flour and stir for about 1 minute. Stir in the hot lobster broth a cup at a time, whisking continuously. When all the broth is incorporated, add the bay leaves, tarragon, celery seed, parsley, and dill. Scrape the vanilla bean seeds into the soup, and simmer for about 30 minutes. Just before serving, add the lobster meat. Garnish with oyster crackers and chives.

We Italians are all so different, but we find ways to remind ourselves that we are a unified country. We have come up with the perfect trinity to express this. When we go out for a casual meal and the bill comes, we say, Ci riunuiamo alla Milanese; si mangia come Toscani con gusto chiaccherie e allegria; e si paga alla Romana *(We come together as* Milanesi*—businesslike and sophisticated; we eat as Tuscans—with a zest for life and spirited chitchat; and we pay as Romans—each one for himself!)*

green vegetable soup

serves 6 to 8

1 butternut squash
1 tablespoon fresh thyme
2 cloves garlic, minced
extra virgin olive oil
salt and pepper
1 medium yellow onion, chopped
1 leek, white part only, cut in 1/2 rounds
1 yellow squash, cut in 1/2 rounds
1 zucchini, cut in 1/2 rounds
1/2 teaspoon celery seeds
8 cups vegetable stock or water
6 cups arugula
6 cups baby spinach
1/2 cup chopped fresh basil
1/2 cup chopped italian parsley

Preheat oven to 425° F.

Peel squash with a vegetable peeler and cut in half lengthwise. Remove seeds and cut in 1-inch cubes. Place squash cubes in a cast-iron pan with thyme, garlic, a drizzle of olive oil, and a pinch of salt and pepper. Add 3/4 cup water and cover pan tightly with foil. Bake for 40 minutes. Remove foil, set oven to broil, and bake another 5 to 10 minutes to caramelize. Remove from oven and set aside.

In a soup pot, sauté onion and leek in olive oil until soft, about 10 minutes. Add yellow squash, zucchini, and celery seeds, and sauté 5 minutes. Add the vegetable stock and simmer about 30 minutes.

Add arugula, spinach, basil, and parsley and let wilt. Transfer half the mixture to a blender and purée. Return purée to soup pot and simmer 10 minutes. Add the roasted butternut squash, salt and pepper to taste, and serve.

italian sausage-barley soup

serves 8 to 10

1 1/2 pounds italian sausage
1 tablespoon chopped garlic
1/4 teaspoon fennel seeds
1/4 teaspoon red pepper flakes
3 cups diced yellow onions
1 1/2 cups diced celery
2 medium carrots, peeled and cut in 1/2 rounds
10 cups chicken stock
8 cups water
1 tablespoon chopped italian parsley
1 cup pearl barley
4 bay leaves

In a soup pot over high heat, cook sausage with garlic, fennel, and red pepper flakes until the sausage begins to brown, about 10 minutes. Drain fat. Add vegetables and cook until onions are translucent. Add chicken stock, water, parsley, barley, and bay leaves. Bring to a boil, then reduce to simmer and cook until barley is soft, about 1 hour and 20 minutes.

tomato-artichoke soup

serves 8 to 10

- 1/2 tablespoon chopped garlic
- 1 red onion, cut in crescents (1 1/2 cups)
- 1 tablespoon extra virgin olive oil
- 1 rind parmigiano
- 2 (14-ounce) cans artichoke hearts, drained and halved
- 3/4 teaspoon basil
- 1/2 teaspoon oregano
- 3 (14-ounce) cans diced tomatoes
- 3/4 cup red wine
- 2 1/2 quarts water
- 2 bay leaves
- 1/2 teaspoon red pepper flakes
- 1/2 tablespoon salt
- 1 teaspoon pepper
- 1/4 cup chopped fresh basil
- 1 tablespoon chopped fresh oregano
- 2 1/2 cups baby spinach, loosely packed
- grated parmigiano

In a soup pot, sauté garlic and onions in olive oil on low heat until onions are translucent. Add parmigiano rind, artichoke hearts, dried basil and oregano, and sauté a few minutes more. Stir in tomatoes, wine, water, bay leaves, red pepper flakes, salt, and pepper. Bring to a boil and simmer 25 minutes.

Add fresh basil, oregano, and spinach. Simmer 5 more minutes. Serve immediately with grated parmigiano.

beef stew

serves 8 to 10

- 3 pounds beef stew meat, cut in 1-inch cubes
- 2 tablespoons chopped fresh thyme leaves, plus extra for garnish
- 2 tablespoons minced garlic
- 1 teaspoon salt
- 1 teaspoon coarsely ground black pepper
- 8 juniper berries
- 4 bay leaves
- 1 small yellow onion, coarsely chopped
- 1/4 cup plus 1 tablespoon extra virgin olive oil, divided
- 3 carrots, peeled and cut in 3/4-inch chunks
- 4 stalks celery, cut in 3/4-inch chunks
- 12 small red potatoes, halved
- 3 ounces butter
- 1/2 cup all-purpose flour
- 2 cups dry red wine
- 4 cups beef stock
- 4 cups water
- 1 pound haricots verts
- 2 cups pearl onions, peeled

In a large mixing bowl, combine beef, thyme, garlic, salt, pepper, juniper berries, bay leaves, onion, and 1/4 cup olive oil. Set aside.

Heat a large soup pot on high heat for a few minutes. When the pot is good and hot, add the marinated beef. Brown the beef for 5 minutes without disturbing. Stir after the meat is browned and caramelized, and continue to brown for another 10 minutes.

Add carrots, celery, potatoes, butter, and flour, and cook for 2 minutes. Stir in the wine, beef stock, and water.

Reduce heat to low, cover, and simmer the stew for at least 3 hours. Stir occasionally, and add more water if stew becomes too thick.

While stew is simmering, blanch haricots verts until soft, about 5 minutes. Set aside. In a skillet, lightly brown pearl onions in 1 tablespoon olive oil, about 2 to 3 minutes.

When the meat is tender, season to taste and add the haricots verts and browned pearl onions. Serve sprinkled with a few thyme leaves.

chicken & wild rice soup

serves 8 to 10

3 tablespoons extra virgin olive oil

2 cups chopped onions

2 cups sliced button mushrooms

2 cups chopped celery

2 cups sliced leeks, white part only, cut in 1/2 rounds

1/2 tablespoon chopped garlic

1 tablespoon dried english mustard

1/2 cup dry sherry

2 tablespoons all-purpose flour

1 gallon chicken stock

4 bay leaves

splash of worcestershire sauce

2 cups wild rice

2 cups shredded chicken

2 cups heavy cream

salt and pepper

Heat olive oil in a soup pot over medium heat, and sauté vegetables, garlic, and mustard until onions are soft. Add sherry and let evaporate. Stir in flour and cook a few more minutes. Add stock, bay leaves, worcestershire sauce, and wild rice. Bring to simmer and cook 45 minutes. Add chicken and cream and simmer until rice is done, another 30 to 45 minutes. Season to taste with salt and pepper.

wedding soup with meatballs

serves 8 to 10

3 quarts chicken stock (p. 59)

4 cups cooked chicken

½ cup grandinina or acini di pepe

½ head escarole, hearts and outer leaves, coarsely chopped

salt and pepper

grated parmigiano

Prepare chicken stock and cooked chicken. When the chicken is cool enough to handle, remove the meat. Add the discarded bones and skin back to the stock, and simmer the broth uncovered for another hour. Shred the picked chicken into small pieces and set aside.

While chicken stock is simmering, make the meatballs.

Pre-cook the grandinina until al dente, rinse with cold water, and set aside.

Strain the chicken stock into a clean soup pot, add the shredded chicken, meatballs, and escarole. Simmer for 15 to 20 minutes. Just before serving, add the cooked pasta to the pot. Season to taste with salt and pepper. Serve with grated parmigiano.

meatballs

makes about 30 (1-inch) meatballs

1 pound ground beef

2 eggs

¼ cup breadcrumbs

½ cup grated parmigiano or pecorino romano

4 tablespoons chopped italian parsley

1 tablespoon fresh oregano

2 cloves garlic, minced

salt and pepper

2 tablespoons all-purpose flour, for dusting

extra virgin olive oil

In a large bowl, thoroughly mix beef, eggs, breadcrumbs, parmigiano, parsley, oregano, garlic, and salt and pepper to taste. Form into 1-inch balls. Dust with flour. In a sauté pan over high heat, add enough olive oil to coat, and brown meatballs on all sides, about 3 minutes.

These meatballs are delicious with spaghetti and tomato sauce, or simply served with sautéed chard. You will want to increase size to 2-inch balls.

Despite its name, this soup is not traditionally served at weddings. Minestra maritata *refers to the harmonious mingling of ingredients—in this case, chicken and meatballs.*

gazpacho

serves 6 to 8

1 english cucumber, peeled and seeded, cut in 1/2 rounds

1 red bell pepper, diced

1 yellow bell pepper, diced

1 small red onion, diced

1/4 cup cilantro leaves

1/4 cup italian parsley leaves

1/2 jalapeño pepper, minced

1 clove garlic, minced

1 (28-ounce) can diced tomatoes

1 (46-ounce) can v-8 or tomato juice

pinch of celery salt

1/2 teaspoon ground coriander

1 teaspoon ground cumin

1 teaspoon chili powder

1 teaspoon tabasco sauce

3 cups diced vine-ripened or heirloom tomatoes

2 tablespoons red wine vinegar

cilantro, radish, or avocado, for garnish (optional)

In a large bowl, combine all ingredients except red wine vinegar and garnish. Place half the mixture in a blender and blend until smooth. Return blended mixture to chopped ingredients and chill for at least 1 hour. Add vinegar just before serving, and garnish as desired.

white bean chili

serves 8 to 10

- 3 cups cannellini beans, soaked overnight in 12 cups water
- 2 teaspoons salt
- 3 bay leaves
- 1/4 cup extra virgin olive oil
- 2 yellow onions, cut in 1/2-inch chunks
- 2 yellow bell peppers, cut in 1/2-inch chunks
- 2 1/2 pounds pork shoulder roast, cut in 1-inch chunks
- 2 tablespoons minced garlic
- 1 1/2 tablespoons chili powder
- 1 tablespoon ground cumin
- 1/2 tablespoon salt
- 1/2 tablespoon ground black pepper
- 1 teaspoon each basil, oregano, thyme, and coriander
- 1/2 teaspoon cayenne pepper
- 4 cups puréed tomatillos, fresh or canned
- 1 cup diced green chilis
- 5 cups chicken stock
- fresh cilantro leaves and chopped green onion, for garnish

Drain and rinse cannellini beans. Place in a large pot with 5 cups cold water, salt, and bay leaves. Bring beans to a boil. Skim the foam that collects on the top. Reduce heat, cover, and simmer until soft, about 3 hours. (This can be done the day before.)

Heat olive oil in a soup pot over medium heat, and sauté onions and peppers for 10 minutes. Add pork, garlic, and all the seasonings. Continue to cook over medium heat until golden brown in color, about 15 minutes. Add the tomatillos, green chilis, and chicken stock. Cover and simmer for 1 hour.

Add the beans with their juices to the chili. Return to a simmer for another 10 minutes, then serve with fresh cilantro and green onion.

spezzatino of beef & kale

serves 8 to 10

3 pounds beef stew meat, cut in 1-inch cubes

8 ounces pancetta, sliced 1/8 inch thick, cut in 1/2-inch squares

1 1/2 tablespoons minced garlic

1/2 teaspoon red pepper flakes

2 teaspoons salt

1 teaspoon peppercorns and 1/2 teaspoon fennel seeds, ground together in spice grinder

1/4 cup extra virgin olive oil

3 onions, cut in thin crescents

2 cups dry white wine

3 russet potatoes, peeled and cut in 1-inch chunks

3 (14-ounce) cans whole italian plum tomatoes, halved, with their juices

10 cups beef stock

2 bunches italian black kale, stems removed and chopped

salt and pepper

In a large mixing bowl, combine beef, pancetta, garlic, and all the seasonings, and set aside.

In a soup pot, heat olive oil over medium-high heat and sauté onions for about 15 minutes, stirring occasionally. Stir in beef and spice mixture, and continue to cook on medium-high heat about 15 minutes. Add wine, potatoes, tomatoes, and stock. Reduce heat, cover, and simmer for 2 1/2 hours. Add the kale, season to taste with salt and pepper, and cook another 30 minutes.

Serve with toasted breads or grilled polenta.

Spezzatino *is a classic* stufato*—a dish cooked in a pot on top of the stove, or* stufa*. The stoves were used both for heating and cooking, and since they were on all day, a pot could be put on in the morning, and hours later the meal would be ready.* Stufati *are cooked, covered, for a long time at very low temperature—a perfect method for tenderizing inexpensive cuts of meat and fish. They are an economical way to serve a large group of people.*

The Basilica di San Giovanni, in the county seat where I was born, served spezzatino *at their regular lunches thanking donors to the church. The music was fabulous, the masses continuous—but of course, the festivities always revolved around food!*

panini

panino alla mortadella di bologna

Two pieces of good bread with a crunchy crust. A smooth and buttery mortadella from Bologna, sliced paper-thin—the real mortadella, with pistachios, secret spices, and a concoction of meats. Crisp and tickling vegetable giardiniera. Two hands (or one), butcher paper, a lunch break and a bench. The tag says "Made in Italy."

Remember that panini *is Italian for sandwich. Cold, hot, grilled, juicy, double-decker, open-faced, freaky, or ridiculous . . . these days,* panini *have endless possibilities. For me, they are about memories and the stuff between two pieces of bread.* Rosette, filoncini, focaccie, baguettes, *and* ciupete*—knock yourself out! But I like to keep it simple.*

muffoletta

serves 6

I loaf ciabatta or other country bread

olive tapenade

1/4 pound sliced provolone

2 balls fresh mozzarella, sliced in 1/8-inch rounds

1/2 pound sliced ham

1/4 pound spicy coppa, sliced paper-thin

1/4 pound sliced salame

Slice the loaf of bread in half horizontally. Spread olive tapenade on both halves. Layer the cheeses and meats on one half, then place the other half on top and press firmly. Slice into 6 triangular pieces.

olive tapenade

I cup pitted kalamata olives

1/2 cup pepperoncini

I teaspoon capers, drained

2 tablespoons red wine vinegar

I clove garlic

2 tablespoons fresh oregano

1/4 cup extra virgin olive oil

In a food processor, blend all ingredients only until chunky.

Salame, coppa, *rich, aged* provolone, *chewy* ciabatta, *a glass of wine. Some flavors are so simple and so good they make me wonder whether I should plan my retirement in Florence around a* panino.

elk burger

makes 6

2 pounds ground elk

1 teaspoon salt

1 teaspoon freshly cracked black pepper

pinch of red pepper flakes

3 roma tomatoes, halved and marinated in extra virgin olive oil, salt and pepper

1 red onion, sliced in 1/4-inch rounds

6 challah buns, sliced in half

6 tablespoons chimichurri

Heat a gas grill 20 minutes on medium-high.

In a mixing bowl, combine elk with salt, pepper, and red pepper flakes. Form the meat into 6 patties about 3/4 inch thick.

Prepare the chimichurri.

When the grill is good and hot, grill tomatoes and onions. Turn after 3 minutes and move to a cooler spot on the grill. Grill burgers 4 minutes on each side for medium-rare. Remove burgers, tomatoes, and onions, and grill the buns about 1 minute. Layer the bun, burger, tomatoes, and onions, and top with chimichurri.

chimichurri

makes about 1/2 cup

1/4 cup minced yellow onion

1 tablespoon minced fresh oregano

4 tablespoons minced italian parsley

1/2 tablespoon crushed pink peppercorns

1 teaspoon salt

2 tablespoons red wine vinegar

1/4 cup extra virgin olive oil

Combine ingredients together in a bowl. Leftover chimichurri can be stored in the refrigerator and used on chicken, beef, or lamb.

egg salad tramezzino

makes 1 pint

8 eggs
1 tablespoon salt
$^1/_4$ cup mayonnaise
1 tablespoon dijon mustard
2 tablespoons pickle relish
$^1/_2$ teaspoon grated horseradish
2 pinches of white pepper
1 tablespoon chopped capers, with juice
butterleaf lettuce
sliced country bread

Place uncooked eggs in enough cold, salted water to cover, then bring to a boil. Turn off heat, cover, and let stand 10 minutes in the hot water. Test one egg for doneness. While still hot, rinse eggs in cold water. Crack and peel, then finely chop.

In a mixing bowl, combine chopped eggs with the remaining ingredients, except lettuce and bread.

Spread egg mixture on sliced bread, add butterleaf, and cut in triangles.

chicken milanese

serves 3

3/4 cup breadcrumbs

1/4 cup grated parmigiano

3 sage leaves

3 (6-ounce) boneless, skinless chicken breasts

salt and pepper

1/2 cup all-purpose flour

2 eggs

1/2 tablespoon dijon mustard

1/4 cup clarified butter (p. 27)

lemon wedges

In a food processor, pulse breadcrumbs, parmigiano, and sage leaves. Set aside.

Split the chicken breasts and pound until they are 1/4 inch thick. Season to taste with salt and pepper, then dredge in flour. In a small bowl, whisk together the eggs and mustard. Dip the chicken, one piece at a time, into the egg mixture, then directly into the breading, pressing firmly to help it stick.

Heat a large sauté pan over high heat. Add the clarified butter (divide in half if you are doing two batches). Place the chicken in the hot pan and fry until crispy and brown, about 1 1/2 minutes. Turn and cook 1 more minute.

Remove from pan and serve with tomato-caper sauce and lemon wedges or in a panino with a few mixed greens.

tomato-caper sauce

1 cup passata di pomidoro sauce (p. 143)

1 tablespoon capers, drained

1 tablespoon chopped italian parsley

Combine all ingredients.

wheat gluten-free ciabatta

makes 1 loaf

1 1/4 cups warm water (105° to 110° F.)

1 3/4 teaspoons sugar

2 teaspoons active dry yeast

1 1/2 cups bob's red mill wheat gluten-free all-purpose flour

2 tablespoons plus 1 teaspoon cornstarch

1/2 teaspoon salt

1 1/2 teaspoons xanthan gum

1 1/2 teaspoons extra virgin olive oil

Preheat oven to 475° F.

In a small bowl, mix water, sugar, and yeast and let stand 5 minutes. In the bowl of a stand mixer with a paddle attachment, combine flour, cornstarch, salt, and xanthan gum. Add yeast mixture and olive oil and mix on medium speed for 8 minutes.

On a sheet pan lined with parchment paper, mound dough in the middle, roughly shaping with a rubber spatula (dough will be very sticky). Sprinkle the top with a little wheat gluten-free all-purpose flour, cover with plastic wrap, and let rise in a warm place until dough has doubled in size, about 30 minutes. Remove plastic wrap.

Reduce oven temperature to 350° F. just as you place the dough into the oven. Bake 25 to 30 minutes, or until loaf is golden brown and sounds hollow when tapped on the bottom.

vegetable burger

serves 6

1 yam, peeled and cut in 1-inch cubes
salt
extra virgin olive oil
1 red bell pepper, finely diced
1/2 sweet yellow onion, finely diced
1/2 jalapeño, minced
3 cloves garlic, minced
1 (15-ounce) can chickpeas, drained and rinsed
1/2 cup chopped fresh cilantro or basil
1 1/2 cups breadcrumbs, divided
pepper
multigrain bread or pita

In a small saucepan, place the yam with enough water to cover halfway, and add a pinch of salt. Cover and cook on low heat until soft, about 30 minutes. Drain.

In a large skillet, heat olive oil over medium-high heat and sauté the pepper, onion, jalapeño, and garlic until soft, about 10 minutes. Set aside.

In a mixing bowl, combine the cooked yam, pepper mixture, and chickpeas, stirring with a fork to combine. Add the cilantro, half the breadcrumbs, and pepper to taste. Divide the mixture into six 1/2-cup scoops. On a baking sheet lined with waxed paper, press scoops into burger shape and refrigerate 30 minutes.

When the burgers have chilled, press both sides in the remaining breadcrumbs. In a large nonstick pan, heat a little olive oil over medium heat. Brown the burgers 6 to 7 minutes, then gently turn and brown for another 5 minutes. Serve with cucumber salsa on toasted multigrain bread.

cucumber salsa

1 1/2 cups chopped cherry tomatoes
1/2 yellow onion, cut in thin crescents
1/2 english cucumber, seeded and chopped
1 tablespoon chopped fresh cilantro or basil
1/3 cup lemon juice
drizzle of extra virgin olive oil
salt and freshly cracked black pepper

Combine all ingredients and refrigerate before serving.

grilled cheese with roasted peppers

makes 6

3 red or yellow bell peppers
extra virgin olive oil
salt and pepper
1 clove garlic, slivered
2 tablespoons chopped fresh basil
1 ½ pounds sliced havarti or cheese of your choice
12 slices country bread
butter, for grilling

Preheat oven to 425° F.

Place the peppers on a baking sheet, drizzle with olive oil, and sprinkle with salt and pepper. Roast in oven 45 minutes, until skin blackens and peppers appear soft. Transfer to a small mixing bowl and cover with plastic wrap. Cool for about 10 minutes, then remove skin and seeds. Marinate the whole peppers with the garlic, basil, and a little more olive oil.

Place the cheese and peppers between two slices of bread. In a large sauté pan on medium heat, add a couple pats of butter and as many sandwiches as you can fit. (Spread a little more soft butter on the topside of the bread while the bottom is cooking.) Cook on low-to-medium heat until golden brown. Flip the sandwiches and partially cover with a lid to help melt the cheese. Cook until other side is golden brown, and repeat with remaining sandwiches. Cut and serve immediately. (You can keep sandwiches hot on a baking sheet in a 350° F. oven until ready to serve.)

I am a minimalist. I eat basic food with good structure. I like to taste all the ingredients. I want real gorgonzola, not foam made of gorgonzola. If it is a good gorgonzola, do not mess with it. Just eat it.

pasta

ziti with cauliflower

serves 8

1 cup golden raisins
1 1/2 cups white wine
2 heads cauliflower (about 2 pounds)
1 pound ziti
4 tablespoons extra virgin olive oil
1 medium white onion, cut in thin crescents
1/4 teaspoon red pepper flakes
3/4 cup toasted pine nuts
1 cup heavy cream
salt and pepper
grated parmigiano

Soak raisins in wine.

Bring a large pot of salted water to a boil. Break cauliflower into florets, reserving outer green leaves, and boil 5 to 7 minutes, until soft. Scoop the cauliflower out of the water with a large slotted spoon and set aside. Let the water continue to boil.

Coarsely chop the outer green leaves of the cauliflower and add to the same pot. Add the ziti.

In a large skillet, heat olive oil over medium-low heat and sauté onions until soft and light gold in color, about 5 minutes. Add the cooked cauliflower and sauté 5 to 6 minutes, or until it gets a little color. Add the raisins, wine, and red pepper flakes and cook a few more minutes. Remove from heat and keep warm.

When ziti is al dente, drain, reserving pasta water. Add the ziti, cooked cauliflower leaves, and 1 cup pasta water to the cauliflower mixture, and cook over high heat for a few minutes. Stir in toasted pine nuts. Add cream and a little more pasta water if you wish.

Season with salt and pepper and toss with parmigiano.

For a lighter pasta, omit the cream and add more pasta water. It's delicious either way!

There is a funny story that demonstrates how Italians are made from a different dough, as we say, from the rest of the world. It involves Signora Agnelli—politician, diplomat, advice columnist, mayor of her Tuscan village, and the first female Italian foreign minister. A blunt, often brusque woman. In reply to a woman who had written to her advice column asking what to do about her husband, who was having an affair with the babysitter, Signora Agnelli replied, "To change a husband is complicated. Changing the babysitter is easier—but next time, remember to get an ugly one! And, if you choose to keep cooking his pasta, that is up to you!"

angel hair with prosciutto cotto & figs

serves 6

2 tablespoons butter

2 tablespoons extra virgin olive oil

1 cup thinly sliced shallots (about 7 medium shallots)

3/4 pound prosciutto cotto, sliced 1/16 inch thick and cut in small squares

1 cup white wine

12 ripe figs, quartered

1 pound angel hair

6 ounces robiola cheese, cut in small squares

1 tablespoon chopped italian parsley

salt and pepper

In a large pot, bring salted water to a boil.

In a wide skillet, heat butter and olive oil. Add shallots and cook over medium heat until tender and lightly browned, about 2 to 3 minutes. Stir in prosciutto and cook 5 minutes more. Add the wine and deglaze pan. Gently stir in figs and remove sauce from heat.

Cook angel hair until al dente. Drain, reserving pasta water. Add pasta to the hot sauce in the skillet and gently toss. Quickly add robiola and 2 cups pasta water, and cook over high heat just long enough to let the flavors blend. Add parsley and salt and pepper to taste, and serve immediately.

In the 12th century, an Arab explorer reported that Sicilians made a pasta called tria, *or "little string." Shaped around knitting needles, the long and stringy pasta was sold from wooden barrels on the streets. It was cooked on the spot and eaten with the fingers. Life would never be the same!*

strozzapreti with sausage & walnuts

serves 6 to 8

1 1/2 pounds ground spicy italian sausage
10 whole sage leaves
1 1/2 cups white wine
1 cup coarsely chopped walnuts
pinch of fennel seeds
pinch of saffron
salt and pepper
3/4 cup heavy cream
pinch of red pepper flakes
1 pound strozzapreti
grated parmigiano

Bring a large pot of salted water to a boil.

In a large skillet over medium-high heat, brown the ground sausage with sage leaves, about 6 minutes. Add the wine and deglaze the pan. Stir in walnuts, fennel seeds, saffron, and salt and pepper to taste, and cook a few minutes longer. Lower heat and stir in cream.

Cook pasta in boiling salted water until al dente. Drain, reserving pasta water.

Add the cooked pasta and 1/2 cup pasta water to the sauce, and toss gently on high heat for a couple of minutes. If needed, add a little more pasta water.

Sprinkle with parmigiano and serve.

The pasta shape strozzapreti, *or "priest-choker," is a long cylinder cinched, or "choked," in the middle. One shape, many stories. I'll tell one of them. My grandfather Angiolo used to say, "Don Pietro, do not eat so fast, or you will choke on that pasta!" Angiolo reflected perfectly the diffuse Tuscan anti-clericalism . . . whereas his wife, Laurina, was the priest's most ardent supporter. So, of course, Don Pietro, as were many caretakers of small dioceses, was invited for lunch every Sunday. Big belly, long black tunic, happy face, rosy cheeks (from the wine), and always hungry. I loved him. He looked forward to a good lunch and good wine, but always ate dangerously fast. So . . . remember to eat this pasta slowly, and go back for seconds!*

naked ravioli with sage butter

serves 6

- 2 pounds spinach
- 15 ounces fresh ricotta, drained on a cheesecloth at least 2 hours or overnight
- 3 egg yolks
- 3/4 cup grated parmigiano, plus extra for serving
- 1/4 teaspoon ground nutmeg
- salt and pepper
- 1/4 cup all-purpose flour for rolling
- 4 ounces butter
- 10 fresh sage leaves

Preheat oven to 350° F.

Bring a wide pot of salted water to a boil. Blanch the spinach 1 to 2 minutes, then remove with a slotted spoon. With your hands, squeeze out water and finely chop. Reserve spinach water.

In a large bowl, combine spinach, ricotta, egg yolks, parmigiano, nutmeg, and salt and pepper to taste. Shape into 2-inch oblong gnocchi. Lightly dust gnocchi in flour and drop into the simmering spinach water a few at a time, cooking until they float, about 2 minutes. Gently remove with a slotted spoon and transfer to a serving tray. Keep warm in the oven until all gnocchi are cooked.

In a small skillet over low heat, melt butter with fresh sage. Lightly press sage leaves while stirring to release flavor. Stir 3/4 cup spinach water into the butter-sage sauce. Pour the sauce over warm gnocchi, top with a sprinkle of parmigiano, and serve.

We Italians are passionate about our gnocchi *and we have a wealth of variations. This particular* gnocchi *is called* malfatti *(not well shaped) or* gnudi *(uncovered, bare, or in my own translation, naked). They can be served with any sauce, but at Cristina's we serve them simply with butter, fresh sage, and parmigiano.*

bavettine alla carrettiera

serves 6

- 1/3 cup extra virgin olive oil
- 1/4 pound speck, thinly sliced and cut in strips
- 5 cloves garlic, slivered
- 1/3 pound cremini mushrooms, sliced
- 1 (14-ounce) can whole san marzano tomatoes, chopped, with their juices
- 1 (10-ounce) can albacore tuna in water, drained
- 1/4 teaspoon red pepper flakes
- 3/4 cup chopped italian parsley, divided
- 1 pound bavettine
- salt and pepper
- 3/4 cup grated pecorino romano

Bring a large pot of salted water to a boil.

In a wide skillet, heat olive oil over medium heat, sauté speck and garlic for a few minutes, until speck is translucent and garlic is lightly browned. Add mushrooms and sauté 1 minute more. Add tomatoes and their juices, tuna, red pepper flakes, and half the parsley. Cook, stirring, 2 to 3 minutes. Set aside.

Cook pasta until al dente. Drain, reserving pasta water. Add the pasta and 1 cup pasta water to the skillet. Toss gently over high heat for a few minutes. Add salt and pepper and remaining parsley. Serve with a drizzle of olive oil and pecorino romano.

The Romans' approach to pasta reflects their preference for earthy simplicity, local produce, loud seasonings, and uncomplicated preparation. Carrettiera *is a traditional Roman pasta—simple, humble, and easy to tweak to your taste. The* carrettieri *were the men who pushed their carts full of produce, meat, chicken, and whatever else they had from the countryside to sell in Rome. Their wives made* carrettiera *during their weekly journey to the capital, often adding mushrooms or other ingredients picked along the way.*

lasagna with radicchio di treviso & taleggio sauce

makes 8 individual lasagnas

3 tablespoons extra virgin olive oil

1 medium yellow onion, finely chopped

1 heart of celery, only tender parts and leaves, cut diagonally in thin slices (about 2 cups)

1/2 pound thinly sliced pancetta, finely chopped

3 heads radicchio di treviso, cut lengthwise in thin strips

1 clove garlic, finely chopped

1 tablespoon fresh thyme, divided

8 fresh lasagna sheets (16 x 3 1/2 inches) rolled thinly

1/2 cup grated parmigiano

salt and freshly cracked black pepper

In a large sauté pan over medium heat, sauté the onion, celery, and pancetta 10 to 15 minutes, until soft and golden. Add the radicchio (reserving 1/2 cup), garlic, and 2 teaspoons thyme, and cook until radicchio is wilted, about 3 minutes. Set mixture aside while you make the taleggio sauce (p. 113).

Preheat oven to 375° F.

Cook lasagna sheets in boiling salted water until al dente. Drain, reserving pasta water.

To assemble the individual lasagnas, spoon enough taleggio sauce to cover the bottom of a 13 x 9-inch baking dish. Place 1 pasta sheet in the baking dish. Arrange 1 tablespoon radicchio mixture on a third of the sheet, drizzle with taleggio sauce, and sprinkle with parmigiano. Loosely fold the empty part of pasta sheet over the mixture. Add a second tablespoon of radicchio mixture and drizzle with taleggio sauce. Repeat one more time. If you like, you can fold the pasta at different angles to create a pinwheel effect. Repeat with the remaining sheets.

Bake the lasagnas 20 minutes, or until the tops are browned and the sauce is bubbly. Just before serving, toss the reserved 1/2 cup uncooked radicchio with a drizzle of olive oil, remaining thyme, and salt and freshly cracked black pepper, and arrange on top of each portion.

continued on page 113

continued from page 111

taleggio sauce

makes about 2 cups

2 ounces butter

2 tablespoons all-purpose flour

1 cup milk

pinch of nutmeg

pinch of white pepper

½ pound taleggio cheese, cut in chunks, rind removed

¾ cup pasta water

Melt the butter on low heat. Whisk in the flour and continue whisking until mixture is a nice golden color, about 2 to 3 minutes. Slowly whisk in milk. Add the nutmeg and white pepper, and whisk over low heat until thickened, about 5 minutes. Stir in cheese until melted. Add reserved pasta water until sauce is smooth and loose.

The long, burgundy-red leaves of radicchio have been a garden staple around Treviso since Medieval times, when it was especially popular among monks, who welcomed anything that would add flavor to their simple diets. Radicchio, like almost everything else in Italy, is seasonal. From December through March, we Italians serve our beloved fiore d'inverno *(winter flower) in lasagnas, risottos, salads, and soups. Our favorite preparation is the simplest: radicchio cut in thin strips, tossed with extra virgin olive oil, and sprinkled with salt and pepper as a salad or a bruschetta topping.*

fusilli with smoked trout

serves 6 to 8

1 1/2 pounds asparagus, cut on diagonal, tough ends removed

1 pound fusilli

2 tablespoons butter

2 tablespoons extra virgin olive oil

1/2 tablespoon minced garlic

2 leeks, cut in 1/2 rounds

juice of 1 lemon

2 cups heavy whipping cream

1 pound smoked trout, in chunks

1/4 cup coarsely chopped fresh dill

2 tablespoons chopped italian parsley

salt and freshly cracked black pepper

grated parmigiano

Bring a large pot of salted water to a boil. Blanch asparagus 1 1/2 minutes and transfer to a bowl. In the same boiling water, add the pasta and cook until al dente.

In a large sauté pan over low heat melt butter with olive oil. Add the garlic and leeks and cook until leeks are soft, about 4 minutes. Add the lemon juice and cream and let simmer. Just before the pasta is done, add the asparagus, trout, dill, parsley, and salt and pepper to the sauce. Drain the pasta, reserving pasta water. Quickly toss pasta in the sauce on high heat, adding pasta water as needed. Serve immediately with grated parmigiano.

Mangia! Mangia! *In Italy we do not typically make plans for dinner with people we know. Our friends just stop by. We get out the* affettati, *we start the water for the pasta, we gossip, we have a glass of wine, and we eat . . . and eat some more.*

cacio e pepe

serves 6 to 8

I pound thin spaghetti

3 ounces freshly cracked black pepper

I cup finely grated pecorino romano

Cook pasta in boiling salted water until al dente. Drain, reserving pasta water. Quickly transfer the pasta to a warm serving bowl. Add the cracked pepper and toss once. Add I cup pasta water and the cheese, mixing only once or twice so the cheese does not clump. Pasta should be brothy and silky. Serve immediately.

Cacio e Pepe *is a dish with a bite that invites you to have a glass of wine. It is a* spaghettata a mezzanote*—a midnight spaghetti feast. An old dish, but still* di moda.

The preparation is all about dexterity and cannot be turned around or corrected. The black pepper must be good quality and neither cracked too fine nor too coarse, but just right. The cheese must dissolve in the pasta water and the pasta must be turned only just enough. The pecorino must be authentic Roman, and excellent. Buon appetito!

campanelle with broccoli & chili oil

serves 6

1½ pounds broccoli

1 pound campanelle

⅓ cup chili oil

5 garlic cloves, slivered

½ cup chopped italian parsley

salt and freshly cracked black pepper

1 cup grated parmigiano

Bring a large pot of salted water to a boil.

Cut broccoli into small florets. Peel stems, slice lengthwise in thin slices and coarsely chop. Place broccoli in boiling water, return to a boil, and cook 1 to 2 more minutes. Add campanelle.

While pasta and broccoli are cooking, heat chili oil in a large skillet. Add garlic and sauté until translucent but not burned. Remove from heat.

Drain pasta and broccoli, reserving pasta water. Add pasta and broccoli to skillet and quickly toss in chili oil over high heat, adding pasta water as needed to keep pasta very moist. Sprinkle with parsley and season to taste with salt and pepper. Transfer to a serving bowl and toss with parmigiano.

chili oil

1 cup extra virgin olive oil

½ jalapeño, halved

1 tablespoon red pepper flakes

a few stems of italian parsley

Combine all ingredients in a small saucepan and heat over medium heat until it sizzles. Remove from heat and let stand for at least 2 hours. Strain and store in a glass container.

rigatoni with beef bolognese

makes 2 quarts

2 ounces dried porcini mushrooms

½ cup extra virgin olive oil

1 yellow onion, minced

1 carrot, minced

2 stalks celery, leaves included, minced

2 cloves garlic, minced

1 cup finely chopped italian parsley

3 pounds ground beef

1 teaspoon salt

1 teaspoon coarsely cracked black pepper

½ teaspoon marjoram

pinch of red pepper flakes

4 cups dry red wine, divided

1 (28-ounce) can plum tomatoes, puréed

3 cups beef stock

3 bay leaves

7 juniper berries

1 pound rigatoni

grated parmigiano

Reconstitute porcini by soaking in 2 cups of hot water for 5 minutes. Squeeze out water, coarsely chop mushrooms, and set aside. Reserve porcini water.

In a large soup pot, heat olive oil over medium-high heat and sauté onion, carrot, celery, garlic and parsley until vegetables are soft, about 8 minutes.

Increase heat to high and add ground beef, salt, and pepper. Allow the beef to brown before stirring, at least 10 minutes. Add the chopped porcini, marjoram, and red pepper flakes and continue to brown, stirring, another 15 minutes.

When the meat begins to stick to the bottom of the pan, add 2 cups wine and scrape the bottom of the pan. Allow all the wine to evaporate. When the beef begins to stick to the pan again, add the rest of the wine, tomatoes, beef stock, reserved porcini water, bay leaves, and juniper berries. Reduce heat and simmer, covered, at least 2 hours.

In a large pot, bring salted water to a boil and cook rigatoni until al dente. Drain, reserving pasta cooking water.

In a large skillet, heat 4 cups of the bolognese. Add cooked rigatoni and gently toss over high heat 2 to 3 minutes, adding a little pasta water if needed. Transfer to a serving bowl and serve with grated cheese.

Bolognese can be stored in the refrigerator for at least 5 days. You can use it to make a delicious lasagna or serve it with grilled ciabatta. It can also be frozen for later use.

Bologna is famous for its fresh pasta and ragu. Ragu *comes from the French* ragoût *and denotes a dish in which small pieces of meat are cooked in a savory sauce. In Tuscany, we call it* sugo. *Dig a fork into a steaming plate of rigatoni with this delicious* sugo *and you will be hooked! No matter what you call it, the secret is slowly cooking the vegetables, adding meat (or not), chicken (or not), broth and livers (or not), and wine, and continuing to cook slowly*—molto piano, piano, piano—*stirring the pot until all the flavors become one.*

David McClung

fish, meat
& vegetables

black cod in salsa verde

serves 6

- 2 pounds black cod, cut in 6 pieces
- 2 cups italian parsley leaves
- 2 cloves garlic
- 1 tablespoon capers, plus 1 teaspoon caper juice
- 1 oil-packed anchovy
- 2 teaspoons red wine vinegar
- $^1/_2$ cup plus 1 tablespoon extra virgin olive oil, divided
- salt and freshly cracked black pepper
- 1 tablespoon finely grated lemon zest
- 6 lemon wedges

Rinse the cod and set aside to dry while you make the salsa verde.

On a cutting board, finely chop the parsley with the garlic, capers, and anchovy. Transfer to a small bowl and stir in the caper juice and vinegar. Stir in 7 tablespoons of the olive oil and season to taste with salt and pepper.

In a bowl, toss the cod with 2 tablespoons of salsa verde.

In a large French skillet, heat the remaining 2 tablespoons olive oil. Add the cod, skin up, and cook over high heat 3 to 4 minutes. Turn the fish and cook 3 more minutes, or until the cod flakes.

Transfer the cod to a warm serving plate, spoon a little salsa verde over the fish, and sprinkle with lemon zest. Serve with lemon wedges.

*We Italians eat a lot of cod, although most of our cod dishes use salted cod (*baccala*), which is inexpensive and sold everywhere. When I was a little girl, I remember going to the market with Quintilia, my grandmother's cook. The vendor would pick up a salted cod fillet from his barrel and wrap it in rough, yellow butcher paper with the tail sticking out the top. As I walked back to my grandmother's house, I would hold the fish as far from me as possible, afraid it might revive at any minute!*

stuffed banana peppers with passata di pomidoro

serves 8

8 medium banana peppers
2 pounds ground italian sausage
1½ cups breadcrumbs
1½ cups grated pecorino romano
½ cup grated parmigiano
½ cup chopped italian parsley
½ cup water
passata di pomidoro sauce (p. 143)

Preheat oven to 350° F.

Slit each pepper lengthwise, leaving the core intact. Remove seeds and place peppers on a baking sheet.

In a large skillet on medium-high heat, brown the sausage about 10 minutes, breaking it into small pieces with a wooden spoon. Remove the sausage from the fat, reserving ½ cup fat.

In a mixing bowl, combine sausage, breadcrumbs, cheeses, and parsley. Add the reserved fat and ½ cup water, and mix together thoroughly.

Stuff the peppers with the sausage mixture. Bake 30 minutes. Serve with passata di pomidoro and extra cheese on top.

My beautiful, funny friend Rosina, a native of Calabria, is the proprietor of a restaurant in San Diego. She has generously shared this recipe with me. According to Rosina, there are three rules for keeping a restaurant in business: 1) Marry money. 2) Marry money. 3) Marry money! Even though neither one of us has managed to do that, we laugh about it . . . and we keep cooking!

pork osso buco with porchetta rub

serves 6

pork osso buco

6 center-cut pork hindshanks osso buco, 2 inches thick, (approximately 3/4 pound each)

2 tablespoons porchetta rub

1/2 cup extra virgin olive oil

2 white onions, cut in 1/4-inch crescents

salt and pepper

2 cups white wine

3 large cloves garlic

4 bay leaves

6 cups chicken stock

Tie each shank with kitchen twine to secure meat to the bone. Rub on all sides with 1 1/2 tablespoons porchetta rub. Refrigerate at least 2 hours or overnight.

Preheat oven to 350° F.

In a large sauté pan, heat 2 tablespoons olive oil over medium-high heat. Add shanks and brown on all sides, about 10 minutes. Remove from heat and set aside.

In a separate sauté pan, heat remaining olive oil. Add onions and salt and pepper to taste, and cook over medium heat, stirring occasionally, until golden and translucent, about 15 minutes. Add the wine and cook 4 to 5 minutes.

Arrange onions in a single layer in a 9 x 12 x 3 1/2-inch baking dish. Add pork shanks, garlic, bay leaves, chicken stock, and enough water to cover the meat.

Cover the baking dish securely with aluminum foil, and bake on lower rack 5 to 5 1/2 hours, or until meat is falling off the bone.

Transfer the cooked meat with a little juice and some onions to a serving platter. Carefully cut off the kitchen twine and discard. Keep the meat warm while you cook the remaining juices over high heat until reduced by half. Pour juices over the meat, sprinkle with remaining 1/2 tablespoon porchetta rub, and serve.

porchetta rub

1 tablespoon fennel seeds

1 tablespoon black peppercorns

1 tablespoon red pepper flakes

1 tablespoon salt

4 cloves garlic, minced (optional)

In a sauté pan, toast fennel seeds over medium heat until slightly darkened and fragrant. Transfer to a spice mill and let cool. Add peppercorns, red pepper flakes, and salt, and grind to medium consistency. If you are using garlic, add only to the amount you will use immediately.

Store remaining rub in a jar to be used later on chicken, fish, or any meat you wish.

Osso buco—*a "bone with a hole." What is in that hole is delicious marrow surrounded by, in this case, pork so tender that you will only need a fork to eat it. Cook this dish the day before serving to deepen its flavor. And do not forget to grill a piece of rustic bread to eat with your marrow.*

veal scaloppine with morels

serves 6 to 8

4 ounces fresh morels or 4 cups dried

1/2 cup all-purpose flour

2 teaspoons salt

1 teaspoon black pepper

2 pounds veal loin, thinly sliced and pounded to 1/8 inch thick, about 16 pieces

1/2 cup extra virgin olive oil

3 sprigs fresh thyme leaves

2 ounces butter, divided

1 1/2 cups dry marsala wine

3 cups chicken stock (substitute half the chicken stock with 1 cup reserved morel water if using dried)

2 tablespoons chopped italian parsley

Slice the larger fresh morels lengthwise and rinse away any dirt. If using dried, reconstitute by soaking in 3 cups of hot water 10 minutes. Squeeze out excess water, reserving water.

Combine flour, salt, and pepper on a baking sheet. Dredge the veal in the seasoned flour, shake off excess, and set aside.

Heat a large skillet over high heat and add enough olive oil to coat the bottom of the pan. Fry the veal quickly, about 30 seconds on each side. Remove from the pan and set aside. In the same pan, add the morels, thyme, and half the butter. Sauté until golden brown, about 3 minutes, then stir in 2 tablespoons of the dredging flour. Reduce heat and slowly add the marsala wine. Let wine evaporate for a minute, then add the chicken stock. Let the sauce reduce until it coats the back of a spoon, about 5 minutes. Add the remaining butter and season with salt and pepper.

Before serving, place the veal in the hot marsala-morel sauce for a minute, and then move to a warm platter. Pour the sauce on top and sprinkle with parsley.

If you like, substitute 2 pounds chicken breast, butterflied and pounded, for the veal.

salmon with brandy-citrus glaze

serves 6

2½ to 3 pounds wild alaskan salmon fillet, pin bones removed

3 sprigs dill leaves

salt and pepper

2 lemons (1 sliced in ¼-inch rounds, 1 sliced in wedges)

Preheat oven to 550° F. Set one rack on the low position and one close to the broiler.

Place salmon on a baking sheet lined with aluminum foil. Sprinkle with dill and salt and pepper to taste, and arrange lemon rounds along the edge of the salmon.

Place the salmon on the lower rack and bake 7 minutes. Remove and brush with 2 to 3 tablespoons of the brandy-citrus glaze. Turn the oven to high-broil and place the salmon on the top rack. Broil 3 minutes. When the salmon is dark and crispy, remove salmon and foil from oven and let rest 5 minutes. Slide a metal spatula under the salmon to pull the fish from the skin, then gently break into 6 portions. Squeeze with fresh lemon wedges and serve drizzled with remaining glaze and yogurt-dill sauce on the side.

brandy-citrus glaze

1½ cups brandy

1 cup fresh orange juice

½ cup honey

In a small saucepan, combine ingredients and simmer about 25 minutes, or until reduced to ¾ cup (watch for flame).

yogurt-dill sauce

1 cup plain greek yogurt

½ cup diced cucumbers

1 tablespoon chopped fresh dill

1 teaspoon lemon juice

pinch of salt and white pepper

In a small bowl, combine all ingredients.

Just for the record, I am not a fan of open kitchens in restaurants. Kitchens are magical places where wild things happen. The mystique should be kept intact.

butterflied leg of lamb with vodka-lemon sauce

serves 6

1 boneless leg of lamb (about 4 pounds)
5 cloves garlic (4 chopped, 1 slivered)
zest of 1 lemon
salt and pepper
4 ounces pancetta, thinly sliced
20 fresh sage leaves, divided
3 tablespoons extra virgin olive oil

On a cutting board, open the lamb. Trim sinew and fat on the inside, while leaving all the fat on the outside. Butterfly and pound the meat to a uniform thickness of about 1 inch. (Have your butcher do this, if you like.)

Arrange chopped garlic, lemon zest, and salt and pepper to taste on the meat. Top with slices of pancetta and 15 sage leaves. Following the grain of the meat, roll lamb up tightly and tie with kitchen string at 2-inch intervals to hold a log shape. Using a small knife, make 1/2-inch-long incisions about 5 inches apart all over the lamb, and insert a sliver of garlic, a sage leaf and salt and pepper into each slit. Drizzle the lamb with olive oil. Cover and refrigerate until ready to grill.

Prepare vodka-lemon sauce.

When ready to cook, transfer lamb to a hot grill and sear on all sides. Turn the heat to medium and cover, turning every 10 minutes, until thermometer inserted into thickest part registers 120° F., about 45 minutes. Transfer to a cutting board and let rest 10 to 15 minutes.

Slice and serve with the sauce.

vodka-lemon sauce

1 large lemon, cut into 1/3-inch-thick slices
3 shallots, thinly sliced
2/3 cup extra virgin olive oil
1 clove garlic, thinly sliced
10 fresh sage leaves
3 tablespoons sugar
2/3 cup dry white wine
1/3 cup lemon vodka
1 cup chicken or beef stock, warmed
salt and pepper

Heat grill to medium-high heat. Grill lemon slices and set aside. In a saucepan, sauté shallots in olive oil until translucent, about 5 minutes. Add garlic, sage leaves, and grilled lemons. Stir in sugar and cook a few minutes to caramelize. Add wine and vodka to deglaze the pan, and flambé. Add warm stock and let simmer a few minutes. Adjust for salt and pepper. Cover and chill. Warm before serving.

Vodka is a fiery drink, not for the faint of heart. It says "I am interested in life; I am in the mood for something warm and exciting!" So try it and let us know.

sautéed spinach, chard & kale

serves 2 to 4

2 pounds spinach, chard, or kale

1 tablespoon extra virgin olive oil

1 clove garlic, thinly sliced

a few drops of lemon juice

Blanch greens in boiling, salted water 2 to 3 minutes for spinach, 8 to 10 minutes for chard and kale. Drain, squeeze out water, and sauté with olive oil and garlic 1 minute. Add a little lemon juice before serving.

If you are not going to use all your greens immediately, squeeze into balls and refrigerate until later.

brussels sprouts with pancetta

serves 6

1 ½ pounds brussels sprouts (about 20)
½ pound pancetta, sliced ⅛ inch thick
2 tablespoons extra virgin olive oil, divided
4 cloves garlic, thinly sliced
pinch of red pepper flakes
salt and pepper
½ cup grated parmigiano

In a small stockpot, bring 10 cups salted water to a boil.

While water is coming to a boil, clean and trim the ends of the brussels sprouts. Remove any outside discolored leaves. Cut the brussels sprouts in half through the core. Blanch about 10 minutes, then drain, reserving ½ cup water.

Chop the pancetta in ½-inch pieces. In a wide sauté pan, heat 1 tablespoon olive oil over high heat. Add the pancetta and stir occasionally until crispy, about 5 minutes. Reduce heat and add the garlic, stirring constantly about 1 minute. Remove pancetta and garlic from pan and set aside, leaving drippings in the pan.

Return the pan to high heat and add the remaining tablespoon of olive oil. Place the sprouts, cut side down, in the pan about 5 minutes without turning. The brussels sprouts will become dark brown and crispy. Use tongs to turn once and let the other side brown.

Toss in the pancetta and garlic, along with a pinch of red pepper flakes. Season to taste with salt and pepper.

Serve in a warm bowl with grated parmigiano.

*It is common practice in our kitchen to double the order of Brussels sprouts every time we cook them . . . because I will eat half! To me, they are like cherries—*uno tira l'altro, *literally, "one will pull the others." You can't eat just one!*

roasted sweet potatoes

serves 6

4 to 5 sweet potatoes
½ teaspoon mustard seeds
10 sage leaves
extra virgin olive oil
salt and freshly cracked black pepper

Preheat oven to 375° F.

Place whole sweet potatoes on baking sheet and roast in oven 1 hour. Remove from oven and allow to cool for a few minutes. Turn oven to broil. When potatoes are cool enough to handle, remove the skins with your fingers. Gently break each potato into two or three chunks and return to baking sheet. Sprinkle with mustard seeds, sage leaves, olive oil, and salt and pepper to taste. Broil 3 to 5 minutes, or until the edges begin to caramelize.

Olive oil goes back to the Romans, of course. It was considered holy, a symbol of peace and fertility. It was also a source of light, a medicine, and—not to be overlooked—a very expensive trading commodity. Rumor has it that olive oil has been sanctified by the Pope for its culinary virtues!

eggplant parmesan

makes 6 stacks

1 large eggplant (1 to 1½ pounds)
salt
extra virgin olive oil
3 cups passata di pomidoro
12 large basil leaves, plus extra for garnish
1½ cups grated mozzarella
1 cup grated parmigiano
freshly cracked black pepper

Preheat oven to 500° F.

Cut the eggplant into ¼-inch-thick rounds to make 18 pieces. Place on a baking sheet and sprinkle a little salt on each piece. Drizzle with olive oil on both sides.

Bake 5 minutes, then turn and bake another 5 minutes. Remove from oven and set aside to cool.

In an ovenproof casserole dish, pour 1½ cups of passata di pomidoro. Arrange eggplant in 6 stacks of 3, alternating eggplant, basil, passata di pomidoro, mozzarella, and parmigiano. Return to oven 5 minutes, or until cheese is golden and bubbly. Top with fresh basil and freshly cracked black pepper. Serve with extra sauce.

passata di pomidoro

makes 5 cups

2 cloves garlic, thinly sliced
¼ cup extra virgin olive oil
2 (28-ounce) cans san marzano whole peeled tomatoes, puréed
¼ teaspoon red pepper flakes
5 basil leaves, chopped
1 tablespoon chopped italian parsley
salt and pepper

In a small saucepan, heat garlic and olive oil over medium heat about 2 minutes, taking care not to burn the garlic. Add the remaining ingredients. When the sauce begins to boil, reduce the heat and simmer about 30 minutes. The sauce should not cook down too much and should stay loose. Add a little water if it becomes too thick.

idaho steak fries

serves 6

4 idaho russet potatoes (about 3 pounds)
2 tablespoons extra virgin olive oil
1 tablespoon paprika
½ tablespoon coarsely ground black pepper
½ tablespoon salt
1 tablespoon fresh thyme leaves

Preheat oven to 375° F.

Wash the potatoes thoroughly in cold water and pat dry. Split in half lengthwise, then cut each half into 8 wedges.

In a large bowl, toss the potatoes with the oil, paprika, pepper, salt, and thyme, making sure the potatoes are evenly coated.

Spread the potatoes on a large baking sheet. Do not crowd or stack the potatoes on each other. Bake 1 hour, undisturbed. The potatoes will be crispy on the outside and soft in the center.

desserts

torta della nonna

makes one 8-inch tart

pastry cream

1/2 vanilla bean
2 cups whole milk
1 strip lemon peel
2 coffee beans
2/3 cup sugar
1 1/2 tablespoons cornstarch
4 egg yolks
1 egg
2 tablespoons butter
1 teaspoon vanilla
1/4 cup pine nuts, for garnish

Cut the vanilla bean lengthwise and scrape seeds into a medium saucepan. Add vanilla bean shell, milk, lemon peel, and coffee beans. Bring to a simmer.

In a medium bowl, mix sugar and cornstarch. Whisk in egg yolks and egg until smooth. Slowly stir in the hot milk mixture. Strain the combined mixture back into the saucepan and cook over medium heat, stirring constantly with a wooden spoon, until thick and bubbly. Stir in butter and vanilla. Set aside to cool. Can be made 3 days ahead. Keep refrigerated.

crust

1 3/4 cups all-purpose flour
1/4 cup plus 2 tablespoons sugar, divided
pinch of salt
pinch of baking powder
4 ounces chilled butter
1 egg
1 egg yolk
1/4 teaspoon vanilla
1 tablespoon marsala wine or water
1/2 tablespoon lemon zest

Preheat oven to 375° F.

In the bowl of a stand mixer with a paddle attachment, add flour, 1/4 cup sugar, salt, and baking powder, and mix until combined. Add in chilled butter and blend until mixture resembles coarse meal. Add egg, yolk, vanilla, marsala wine, and zest, and mix just until dough comes together. Transfer dough to a lightly floured surface and roll out one-half the dough into a 10-inch circle. Ease into a buttered and lightly floured 8-inch tart pan with a removable bottom. Press the dough into the bottom and along the sides.

Pour cooled pastry cream into the crust, mounding it in the center. Roll out the remaining half of the dough into a 10-inch circle. Gently place it on top of the pastry cream and press around the edge of the tart pan, cutting off excess dough. Brush the top of the tart with egg wash (p. 151) and sprinkle with pine nuts and the reserved 2 tablespoons sugar. Bake 30 to 35 minutes, or until golden brown.

continued on page 151

continued from page 149

egg wash

1 egg
2 tablespoons water

Whisk together egg and water until blended.

Le nonne *(the grandmothers) used to bake these cakes for the children. Although it was always the same basic cake, they called it something different each time. Eventually the children figured out that the cakes were the same and only the fillings were different—jam one day, apples the next day,* crema *on Sunday, and so on. But they never said anything because they were afraid the grandmothers would stop making the cakes for them.*

I can eat this entire torta *all by myself.* Buonissima *when still warm! Just as good served with* vino santo *at dinnertime.*

chocolate tartufo

serves 6

1/4 cup sugar

2 tablespoons water, room temperature

2 egg yolks

1 tablespoon sifted cocoa powder, plus extra for dusting

1/2 cup dark chocolate (70% or more cacao)

1/2 teaspoon saba wine syrup

2/3 cup heavy cream

In a heavy saucepan, dissolve sugar in water over medium-low heat until temperature reaches 108° F.

In the bowl of a stand mixer with a whisk attachment, whip egg yolks with the sugar syrup. Mix in 1 tablespoon cocoa powder.

In a double boiler, melt chocolate with saba, then transfer to a bowl.

Fold egg and sugar mixture into the melted chocolate.

Whip heavy cream to soft peaks and fold into chocolate mixture. Refrigerate overnight or until set, 1 to 2 hours.

When ready to serve, line a baking sheet with parchment paper. Place six scoops of chocolate mixture onto the parchment paper and dust with cocoa powder. Transfer scoops onto chilled dessert plates, surround with a drizzle of chocolate sauce, and serve.

chocolate sauce

2 cups sugar

1 cup cocoa powder

pinch of salt

1 can evaporated milk

4 ounces butter

2 tablespoons coffee liqueur

1/2 teaspoon vanilla

Place sugar, cocoa powder, and salt in a large saucepan. Whisk in the remaining ingredients and heat over low heat, stirring, until dissolved. Bring to a boil and remove from heat.

Always eat the real thing. Forget the chemically engineered "foods" with their pretense of keeping you healthy. Forget the chocolate-flavored topping! Forget the fake sweetener. Say yes to butter, to chocolate, and to sugar. Keep it real, keep it simple, keep it naked.

double chocolate brownies

makes 16

5 ounces unsweetened chocolate

10 ounces softened butter

2 1/2 cups sugar

5 eggs, room temperature

2 teaspoons vanilla

1 1/4 cups all-purpose flour

1 teaspoon salt

3/4 cup roughly chopped pecans

3/4 cup chocolate chips

Preheat oven to 350° F.

In a double boiler over low heat, melt unsweetened chocolate, stirring occasionally. When chocolate is melted, set aside.

In the bowl of a stand mixer with a paddle attachment, cream butter and sugar. Add eggs, vanilla, and melted chocolate and mix until just combined. Remove bowl from mixer and fold in flour and salt.

Pour batter into a buttered 10 x 10-inch pan, mounding it slightly in the middle. Sprinkle with pecans and chocolate chips. Bake 20 to 25 minutes, or until a toothpick inserted in the center comes out clean. Let cool, then cut into the size you like.

I don't typically eat at home, but if I do, it's chocolate.

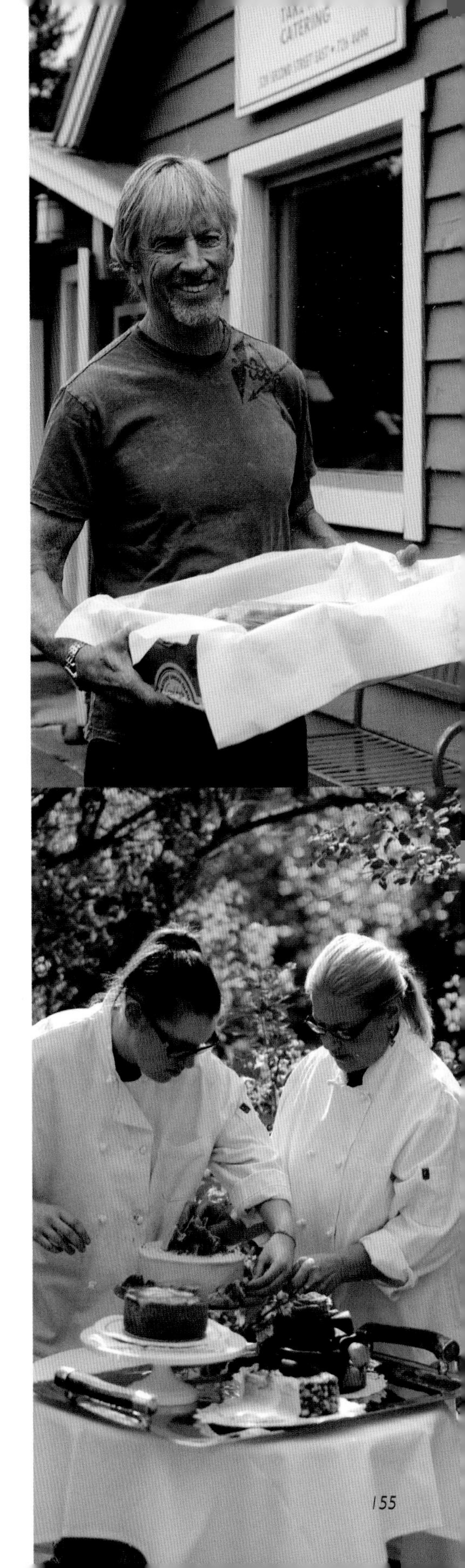

wheat gluten-free brownies

makes 16

1 cup sugar
3/4 cup garbanzo bean flour
1/2 cup cocoa powder
1/4 cup potato starch
1/4 cup tapioca starch
2 tablespoons arrowroot
2 teaspoons baking powder
1/4 teaspoon baking soda
1/2 teaspoon xanthan gum
1 teaspoon salt
1/2 cup coconut oil
1/2 cup applesauce
1 tablespoon vanilla
1/2 cup hot coffee or water
1/2 cup mini chocolate chips

Preheat oven to 350° F.

Butter an 8 x 8-inch pan. In the bowl of a stand mixer with a paddle attachment, combine dry ingredients. Add coconut oil, applesauce, vanilla, and hot coffee or water. Beat until smooth, about 10 minutes.

Spread the batter in the pan and sprinkle with chocolate chips. Bake 18 minutes, or until a toothpick inserted in the center comes out with crumbs on it. Let cool and cut into small squares.

612

coconut cream pie

makes one 9-inch pie

crust

2 cups all-purpose flour

1/2 teaspoon salt

7 ounces chilled butter, cubed

2 tablespoons ice water

In the bowl of a food processor, mix flour and salt. Add the butter pieces and process until the mixture resembles coarse meal. Add the ice water and mix until the dough just holds together. Form dough into a ball, wrap in plastic, and refrigerate 30 minutes.

Roll the chilled dough to form a 12-inch circle. Place in a 9-inch tart pan buttered and dusted with flour, trim edges, and chill about 20 minutes.

Preheat oven to 350° F.

Line the crust with foil, pressing it gently into the corners and edges, and cover it with dried beans or pie weights. Bake until edges begin to color, about 20 minutes. Remove beans and foil and continue to bake until the crust turns a rich, golden color. Cool completely on a rack before filling.

coconut cream filling

1 package knox gelatin

1/4 cup milk

1 cup sugar

2 tablespoons cornstarch

3 egg yolks

2 1/2 cups heavy cream, divided

1/2 vanilla bean, seeds scraped out

1/2 teaspoon pure coconut extract

1/4 cup shredded coconut

In a small bowl, dissolve gelatin in the milk. Set aside.

In a large bowl, whisk together sugar and cornstarch. Add egg yolks and 1/4 cup heavy cream, and whisk until smooth. Set aside.

In a saucepan bring 3/4 cup heavy cream and vanilla bean and seeds to a boil. Slowly add the heated cream to the egg yolk mixture, whisking constantly. Strain mixture back into the saucepan, and bring to a boil over medium heat until thickened. Remove from heat and stir in gelatin mixture and coconut extract until dissolved. Refrigerate overnight.

In a stand mixer with a whisk attachment, mix the cold coconut cream on medium speed until smooth. Add remaining 1 1/2 cups heavy cream and whip until thick, scraping down the bowl as needed. Fold in the shredded coconut. Spoon into pie crust, mounding the cream in the center.

Cover the coconut cream with whipped cream and sprinkle with toasted coconut flakes. Chill pie about 1 hour before serving.

whipped cream

2 cups heavy cream

3 tablespoons powdered sugar

1/4 cup toasted coconut flakes*

In a stand mixer with a whisk attachment, whisk cream and sugar to form stiff peaks.

* To toast coconut flakes, heat in a 375° F. oven 2 1/2 to 3 minutes.

granita al caffè

serves 8

1/2 cup sugar
1 3/4 cups water
3 cups strong coffee
1 tablespoon instant espresso
pinch of ground espresso, for garnish
chocolate-covered coffee beans, for garnish
1 cup whipped cream for topping (p. 159)

Combine sugar and water in a saucepan. Bring to a boil, stirring, until sugar is dissolved, about 6 minutes. Remove simple syrup from heat and chill.

Add the instant espresso to the coffee and cool.

Pour chilled coffee into a 9 x 11 x 2-inch pan. Stir in simple syrup and freeze 45 minutes. Using a wooden spoon, scrape any ice formed on the sides into the rest of the mixture. Repeat every hour for 3 to 4 hours, scraping until mixture resembles crushed ice.

Before serving, fluff the granita with a wooden spoon. Scoop into chilled glasses, top with a dollop of whipped cream, a pinch of ground espresso, and a chocolate-covered coffee bean.

Make this granita as strong as you like by adding more espresso.

In no other country but Italy does social life revolve so much around coffee. Always freshly ground and prepared, the perfect cup is almost black, hidden beneath a light brown layer of froth, or crema.

In the summer months, everyone turns out for la passeggiata *(the evening stroll), where courtship and friendship are celebrated. Enjoy this granita while walking or sitting by the river. It will lift and soothe your spirit.*

creamy cheesecake

makes one 9-inch cake

crust

2½ cups graham cracker crumbs
4 ounces butter, melted
2 teaspoons vanilla

Preheat oven to 350° F.

In a bowl, combine all ingredients and mix well. Press the mixture into the bottom and sides of a 9-inch springform pan. Bake 10 minutes, then set aside to cool.

filling

3 pounds cream cheese, room temperature
1½ cups sour cream
1¼ cups sugar
1 tablespoon vanilla
1 tablespoon cornstarch
3 eggs

Fill a baking pan with water and place on the bottom of the oven.

In a food processor, blend the cream cheese until smooth and free of lumps. Add sour cream, sugar, vanilla, and cornstarch, and blend 1 minute. Scrape down the sides, then add eggs and mix until just incorporated.

Pour mixture into cooled graham cracker crust and bake 1 hour. Turn off heat, leaving oven door open about 2 inches. Let cheesecake rest in the oven 1 more hour, then remove and cool. Refrigerate overnight before releasing from the springform pan.

blueberry cobbler

serves 6 to 8

filling

5 cups fresh blueberries

1/3 cup sugar

2 tablespoons lemon juice

2 tablespoons plus 2 teaspoons cornstarch

1/2 cup cold water

topping

1 1/4 cups flour

pinch of salt

1 1/2 teaspoons baking powder

3 ounces chilled butter, cut in 1/4-inch pieces

2/3 cup heavy cream, plus extra for brushing

3 tablespoons sugar, for sprinkling

Preheat oven to 350° F.

In a saucepan over medium heat, combine blueberries, sugar, and lemon juice. Bring to a boil, stirring occasionally. Whisk cornstarch into cold water until completely dissolved. Add to blueberries and cook until mixture returns to a boil, about 3 minutes.

In the bowl of a stand mixer with a paddle attachment, mix flour, salt, and baking powder. Add cold butter and mix until it resembles coarse meal. Add cream and mix until just combined.

Pour hot blueberry mixture into an 8-inch deep-dish pie pan. Cover the surface of the blueberry mixture with clumps of topping. Brush the top with cream and sprinkle generously with sugar. Bake 30 to 45 minutes.

sbrisiolona

serves 8 to 10

2 cups sliced almonds, finely crushed

1 1/2 cups all-purpose flour

1 1/4 cups cornmeal

1 1/4 cups powdered sugar or 2/3 cup granulated

2 egg yolks

zest of 1 lemon

1/4 teaspoon salt

1 teaspoon vanilla

1 cup butter, softened

1/2 cup sliced almonds, for topping

Preheat oven to 350° F.

In a large bowl mix crushed almonds, flour, and cornmeal. Make a well in the center and add powdered sugar, egg yolks, lemon zest, salt, and vanilla. Stir in softened butter and lightly mix only until the dough is crumbly.

Butter two 9-inch tart pans. Crumble mixture into pans. Dough should be uneven, not pressed down. Sprinkle with sliced almonds.

Bake about 35 minutes, or until golden brown.

It is not a cake, a tart, or a torte. So what is it? It is the crunch de la résistance! *A crunchy, crumbly . . . something. A blend of simple ingredients with lots and lots of almonds. Break it with your hands and serve with whipped cream,* crème anglaise, gelato, *or dangerously just the way it is. Presented in a tin, it's the perfect gift.*

candied orange peels dipped in chocolate

makes about 1 pound

8 valencia oranges

18 cups water, divided

5 cups water

6 cups sugar, plus extra for coating

3/4 cup corn syrup

1/4 cup grand marnier

Score orange peel into 6 sections and remove from the orange. Slice peels lengthwise into 1/4-inch strips.

In a saucepan, bring 6 cups water to a boil. Drop the orange peels into the boiling water and return to a boil. Drain the peels. Repeat this process two times more, using fresh water each time.

Place 5 cups water, sugar, and corn syrup in a saucepan. Stir well and bring to a boil. Add the orange peels, return to a boil, then simmer on low heat about 1 hour and 20 minutes, or until peels begin to look translucent. Remove from heat and let peels sit in the syrup overnight.

Drain the peels, place on a baking sheet, and let rest a second night in a cool place.

Brush the peels with grand marnier. Sprinkle with sugar, and gently toss the baking sheet to thoroughly coat the peels.

Line a baking sheet with parchment paper. Temper the chocolate. Dip 1/3 the length of each peel in the tempered chocolate. Place the dipped peels on the parchment paper and allow the chocolate to harden before serving.

tempered chocolate

9 ounces good bittersweet chocolate, chopped and divided (scharffen berger 70% cacao or valrhona 71% cacao)

In a double boiler, heat water to a simmer. Turn off the heat, and place 6 ounces of chopped chocolate in the top of the double boiler. Let chocolate melt to exactly 115° F., stirring occasionally. If chocolate does not melt to 115° F., turn heat on very low until it does.

Stir the remaining 3 ounces of chopped chocolate into the melted chocolate until completely melted. Remove pan and set aside.

Discard water from double boiler and bring new water to 90° F. Place the melted chocolate over the 90° F. water. When the temperature of the chocolate falls to 86° to 89° F., it is ready for dipping. If the temperature falls below 86° F., you may have to add a little hot water to the pan beneath the chocolate. Be careful not to let any water get into the chocolate.

Use immediately for dipping.

When I was a child, the sweet things we ate revolved around the year like a merry-go-round—they changed with the seasons. Winter brought warm zabaione, quince, and candied orange peels. We knew the holidays were coming when the orange peels appeared. We would creep into the kitchen in our pajamas and slippers and take them in our little hands. They were gone in two bites!

honeycomb

serves 8 to 10

1 1/2 cups sugar

2 tablespoons water

1/4 cup coffee liqueur

1/4 cup light corn syrup

3 teaspoons baking soda

In a deep saucepan, stir together sugar, water, liqueur, and corn syrup. From this point on, the mixture needs to be left alone—no mixing, no stirring, no touching! Bring to a boil. While the sugar is boiling, use a pastry brush dipped in hot water to carefully brush the sides of the pan so the sugar crystals fall back into the mixture. Cook on medium-high heat to the hard crack stage (310° F. on a candy thermometer), about 10 to 15 minutes.

Remove from heat and add baking soda. The mixture will foam rapidly. Stir briskly until mixture thickens, taking care not to break down foam with excessive stirring.

Pour mixture into an ungreased 9 x 9-inch pan. Do not stir. Let stand until cool, then knock the honeycomb out of the pan and break into coarse pieces.

Serve honeycomb as is with ice cream, drizzled with warm chocolate ganache, with whipped cream . . .

chocolate ganache

3/4 cup semisweet chocolate chips

1/3 cup heavy cream, warmed

In a double boiler, melt the chocolate chips. Stir in the warm cream until the mixture is smooth and shiny.

We Italians call them i peccati di gola, *or "little indulgences"—small things to offer, to be gifted, but also to be eaten (maybe without telling) to console or comfort ourselves. The excuse to prepare liqueurs and* dolcezze *was, and is, always the same: should someone come to visit, there is something in the house to offer. But if no one comes, of course, we can't waste them . . . so we have an excuse to eat them!*

limoncello spritzer

makes 1 drink

3 shaves fresh ginger
1 ounce limoncello
1 ounce gin
club soda
twists of lemon, for garnish
juniper berries, for garnish

In a cocktail shaker, muddle the ginger. Fill shaker with ice, then add limoncello and gin. Shake for a few seconds, then strain over ice in a glass. Add a splash of club soda and garnish with a twist of lemon and a juniper berry. For the holidays, add cranberries or red currants. For summer, add a couple of wild strawberries.

If you want to make your own limoncello, my family recipe can be found in my first cookbook, Cristina's of Sun Valley.

chocolate-raspberry tart

makes one 9-inch tart

crust

1¾ cups flour

⅓ cup sugar

¼ teaspoon salt

6 ounces chilled butter, cut in small cubes

1 egg yolk

1 teaspoon vanilla

chocolate ganache (p. 171)

2 pints fresh raspberries

raspberry glaze

30 dark chocolate coins (optional)

In the bowl of a stand mixer with a paddle attachment, combine flour, sugar, and salt. Add butter and mix until the mixture resembles coarse meal. Add egg yolk and vanilla, and mix on medium-high speed until dough comes together in a ball. Remove, wrap in plastic, and refrigerate at least 30 minutes.

On a lightly floured surface, roll the chilled dough to form a 10-inch circle. Ease into a lightly buttered and floured 9-inch tart pan with a removable bottom. Press the dough into the bottom and along the sides. Prick the bottom with a fork, and chill 20 minutes.

Preheat oven to 350° F.

Bake the crust 15 to 17 minutes, or until done. Cool completely on a rack before filling.

Prepare chocolate ganache. Pour into cooled tart shell and refrigerate until slightly set, about 10 minutes. Starting at the outer edge, place raspberries on ganache until the tart is completely covered. Refrigerate while you prepare the raspberry glaze.

raspberry glaze

¼ cup seedless raspberry or apricot jam

3 tablespoons water or your favorite liqueur

In a small saucepan, bring the jam and water to a boil. Stir until mixture is smooth. With a pastry brush, gently brush the tops of the raspberries with glaze. Decorate the edge of the tart with chocolate coins.

chocolate thingy

serves 8 to 10

- 1 cup sugar, divided
- 2 cups half-and-half
- 7 egg yolks
- 1 1/2 cups chocolate chips, divided
- 1 1/2 teaspoons vanilla
- 8 cups leftover chocolate cake chunks and broken chocolate cookies
- 1/2 cup walnut halves

Preheat oven to 350° F.

In a saucepan, bring 1/2 cup sugar and the half-and-half to a boil.

In a medium bowl, whisk egg yolks with remaining 1/2 cup sugar. Slowly add hot half-and-half mixture to egg yolk mixture, whisking constantly. Add 1 cup chocolate chips and vanilla, and stir until chocolate is melted.

In a buttered 8-inch deep-dish pie pan, add cake and cookie pieces. Pour the chocolate mixture over pieces and sprinkle with remaining 1/2 cup chocolate chips and walnuts. Loosely cover with foil and bake until set, about 1 hour.

CRISTINA'S
of Sun Valley
Marionberry Jam

breakfast

pumpkin-cranberry muffins

makes 8

1 cup all-purpose flour
1 cup whole wheat flour
1/4 teaspoon salt
2 teaspoons baking powder
1/4 teaspoon baking soda
3/4 teaspoon cinnamon
1/2 teaspoon ginger
1/4 teaspoon nutmeg
1/4 cup packed brown sugar
1/2 cup sugar
3/4 cup dried cranberries
3/4 cup chopped walnuts
2 eggs
3/4 cup canned pumpkin purée
1 teaspoon vanilla
1 tablespoon vegetable oil
1/4 cup buttermilk
4 ounces unsalted butter, melted
1/4 cup sunflower seeds, for topping

Preheat oven to 350° F.

In a large bowl, mix together dry ingredients and set aside. In a separate bowl, whisk together eggs, pumpkin, vanilla, oil, buttermilk, and butter.

Stir the liquid mixture into the dry ingredients until just incorporated.

Mound the dough above the rim in lightly buttered muffin tins. Sprinkle with sunflower seeds and bake 20 minutes.

frittata with potatoes & onions

makes 1 serving

7 small red new potatoes (about 1 cup)

1/2 tablespoon extra virgin olive oil

1 tablespoon butter, divided

1/4 medium white onion, cut in thin crescents (about 1 cup)

1/4 teaspoon crushed mustard seeds

1/4 teaspoon dried or pinch of fresh marjoram

salt and pepper

3 eggs

1/3 cup water

greens (optional)

cobb vinaigrette (p. 53), optional

Place potatoes in cold, salted water and boil until cooked but firm, about 20 to 25 minutes. Drain and set aside.

In an 8-inch egg pan, heat olive oil and 1/2 tablespoon butter on low heat. Add onions and sauté, stirring occasionally, until very lightly browned.

Cut potatoes into 1/8-inch-thick slices and add to the onions. Stir in mustard seeds, marjoram, and salt and pepper to taste, and cook a few minutes longer on medium-low heat to flavor the potatoes.

In a bowl, whisk together eggs and water. Pour over the potatoes and cook on medium heat, lifting eggs from the side of the pan with a rubber spatula until the bottom firms. Place a plate over the pan and flip the fritatta onto the plate. Add remaining 1/2 tablespoon butter to the pan, and slide the fritatta back in; let firm a few minutes more.

If you like, top with a handful of your favorite greens tossed in cobb vinaigrette.

orange-cinnamon french toast with devon cream & amarene

serves 6

10 eggs

1 cup heavy cream

1 tablespoon cinnamon

1 teaspoon nutmeg

2 tablespoons vanilla

1 cup water

12 slices orange-cinnamon bread, about 3/4 inch thick (p. 187)

4 1/2 tablespoons butter, divided

devon cream

amarene in syrup

powdered sugar, for dusting

In a mixing bowl, whisk together eggs, cream, cinnamon, nutmeg, vanilla, and water. Pour into a baking dish.

Soak each side of bread in the egg mixture for 30 seconds. In a large skillet over medium heat, melt 3/4 tablespoon butter for each 2-slice serving. Cook 3 1/2 minutes on each side, or until golden brown. Repeat with remaining slices.

Serve with a dollop of devon cream, a tablespoon of amarene in syrup, and a dusting of powdered sugar.

You know you are a grown-up when French toast becomes your dinner of choice. You eat it not because there is nothing else in the house . . . but because you like it.

orange-cinnamon bread

makes two 9 x 5-inch loaves

1 1/2 tablespoons active dry yeast

pinch of sugar

1/4 cup warm water (105° to 115° F.)

1 cup warm whole milk (105° to 115° F.)

1 cup orange juice

1/2 cup sugar

4 tablespoons unsalted butter, melted

2 eggs

grated zest of 2 oranges and 1 lemon

2 teaspoons salt

6 1/2 cups unbleached all-purpose or bread flour, divided, plus more for kneading

2 tablespoons unsalted butter, melted, for brushing

2/3 cup sugar mixed with 1 1/2 tablespoons cinnamon

In a small bowl, sprinkle the yeast and pinch of sugar over the warm water. Stir to dissolve and let stand until foamy, about 10 minutes.

In a large bowl of a stand mixer with a paddle attachment, combine the milk, juice, sugar, butter, eggs, zest, salt, and 2 cups of the flour. Beat until smooth, about 1 minute. Add the yeast mixture and 1 cup more flour. Beat 1 minute more. Add the remaining flour 1/2 cup at a time to form a soft dough that just clears the sides of the bowl.

Transfer dough to a lightly floured surface and knead until smooth and springy, about 3 minutes, adding 1 tablespoon of flour at a time as needed to prevent sticking. Place in a well-oiled large bowl, turning once to coat the top, and cover with plastic wrap. Let rise in a warm place until doubled in bulk, about 1 to 1 1/2 hours.

Turn the dough out onto the work surface and divide into 2 equal portions. Roll each portion into a thick rectangle about 8 x 12 inches. Brush the surface of each rectangle with melted butter and sprinkle with half the cinnamon sugar, leaving a 1-inch border around the edges. Roll up jelly-roll fashion from the short end to form a loaf shape. Pinch the seams to seal completely. Place each loaf seam-side down in a buttered 9 x 5-inch loaf pan. Cover loosely with plastic wrap and let rise at room temperature until 1 inch above the rims of the pans, about 45 minutes.

Twenty minutes before baking, preheat oven to 350° F.

Bake in the center of the oven until bread is golden brown and sounds hollow when tapped, about 40 to 45 minutes. Remove from pans and cool on a rack before slicing.

This bread makes a very special toast. You can vary the flavor and color by experimenting with different oranges—navels or Valencias, blood oranges, even mandarins or tangerines.

mr. c's eggs

serves 6

1 clove garlic, slivered
1/4 cup extra virgin olive oil
3 cups fresh diced tomatoes
1 1/2 cups passata di pomidoro (p. 143)
6 leaves fresh basil, torn in small pieces
6 poached eggs (p. 49)

In a large skillet, sauté garlic in olive oil until light golden brown. Add fresh tomatoes and cook over medium heat about 4 minutes. Add passata di pomidoro, and simmer over low heat until ready to serve.

Poach eggs. Divide the sauce in 6 small bowls and top with basil leaves. Nestle one poached egg in the sauce of each bowl.

breakfast pizza

makes 1 serving

1 pizza skin (p. 33)
1/4 cup passata di pomidoro (p. 143)
3/4 ball fresh mozzarella
4 strips crispy bacon, chopped in bits
fresh oregano leaves
3 eggs, beaten with a fork
extra virgin olive oil
freshly cracked black pepper

1 pizza skin (p. 33)
1/4 cup passata di pomidoro sauce (p. 143)
1/4 pound aged provolone, shaved
1/4 pound thinly sliced ham, chopped
6 basil leaves, chopped
2 to 4 eggs, fried, scrambled or poached
extra virgin olive oil
freshly cracked black pepper
red pepper flakes

Choose pizza ingredients. Preheat oven to 500° F. and place a rack in the middle.

Spread the passata sauce on the pizza skin. Tear the mozzarella into small pieces and arrange on top of the sauce. Sprinkle with bacon and oregano, and place directly on the oven rack. Bake 5 to 7 minutes, until cheese is bubbly and crust is golden. While the pizza is cooking, warm a drizzle of olive oil in an egg pan over medium-high heat. Add the eggs and reduce heat. Gently stir eggs with wooden spoon until just set, about 2 minutes. When pizza is done, top with scrambled eggs. Cut into quarters, drizzle with olive oil, and top with freshly cracked black pepper.

The word pizza *comes from the Latin* pinsere, *"to flatten or push down." The first written recipe dates from 1858, and reads, "Take a piece of dough, flattened with a* matterello *[rolling pin]. Arrange on top what comes to your mind. Drizzle with olive oil or lard. Cook in an oven and eat it. If you do not have an oven, fry it."*

12 OZ

crunchy granola

makes about 7 cups

1 1/3 cups mixed dried fruits (golden raisins, diced apricots, cranberries, cherries)

4 cups rolled oats

1 2/3 cups mixed nuts (pecans, walnuts, slivered almonds, hazelnuts, cashews)

2/3 cup raw unsweetened coconut flakes

1/2 cup honey

2 1/2 tablespoons molasses

1/4 cup vegetable oil

1 teaspoon vanilla

Preheat oven to 350° F.

Arrange the dried fruit on a baking sheet and place in the oven 5 minutes. Stir, then turn oven off and leave fruit to dry in the oven at least 2 hours.*

Preheat oven again to 350° F.

Combine oats, nuts, and coconut flakes, and spread out on a baking sheet.

In a saucepan over low heat, warm the honey, molasses, oil, and vanilla. Pour over oat mixture and mix well to thoroughly coat.

Bake on the lower rack, stirring every 5 minutes, for 20 minutes, or until granola is a deep golden color.

Remove from oven and break apart the large clumps. Allow granola to cool at room temperature, uncovered, stirring occasionally. Mix in the dried fruit. Do not refrigerate.

* Dried fruit can be prepared up to three days ahead and left uncovered at room temperature.

belgian waffles with panna cotta & macerated strawberries

makes 6 to 8 waffles

3 cups all-purpose flour
1 tablespoon baking powder
1 teaspoon salt
1 1/2 tablespoons sugar
1/2 tablespoon cinnamon
6 eggs, separated
3 cups milk
8 ounces melted butter, cooled
2 tablespoons turbinado sugar
powdered sugar, for dusting

Sift together all dry ingredients.

In a bowl, whip egg whites into stiff peaks and set aside. In a separate bowl, whisk together milk and yolks.

Add milk mixture to dry ingredients. Stir in cooled butter, then gently fold in whipped egg whites and turbinado sugar.

Pour into a waffle iron and cook. Serve with a dollop of panna cotta and macerated strawberries.

panna cotta

makes 8 to 10 servings

2 1/4 teaspoons knox gelatin
1/3 cup whole milk
2 1/4 cups heavy cream, divided
1/4 cup sugar
pinch of salt
1 vanilla bean

In a small dish, sprinkle gelatin on milk and let sit until it blooms.

In a saucepan, whisk together 1 1/4 cups cream, sugar, and salt. Split the vanilla bean lengthwise and scrape the seeds into the cream and sugar, then drop in the shell. Bring to a boil. Remove from heat and discard vanilla bean shell. Stir in gelatin mixture until it dissolves. Let cool.

Whip the remaining 1 cup cream until it forms soft peaks, then fold into the cream mixture. Pour into a 1-quart bowl and refrigerate at least 4 hours or overnight.

macerated strawberries

3 cups strawberries, sliced
1/2 cup sugar
juice of 1/2 lemon

Toss ingredients and let sit at least 30 minutes.

Metric Conversion Chart

Volume Measurements

U.S.	Metric
1 teaspoon	5 ml
1 tablespoon	15 ml
1/4 cup	60 ml
1/3 cup	75 ml
1/2 cup	125 ml
2/3 cup	150 ml
3/4 cup	175 ml
1 cup	250 ml

Weight Measurements

U.S.	Metric
1/2 ounce	15 g
1 ounce	30 g
3 ounces	90 g
4 ounces	115 g
8 ounces	225 g
12 ounces	350 g
1 pound	450 g
2 1/4 pounds	1 kg

Temperature Conversion

Fahrenheit	Celsius
250	120
300	150
325	160
350	180
375	190
400	200
425	220
450	230

I love storytelling with its colors, romance, and the European fairy tale ending, "And they lived happily ever after."

It happened in Sun Valley . . . con amore!